Stoic Indifference

Manual of Basic Mental Discipline

Fausto DiCampo

Contents

Prologue..4

Chapter 1: Philosophy as basis for mental discipline...............8

Introduction..9

Stoicism..21

Application of Stoicism..44

Stoic advice and aphorisms..56

Rationalization...70

Habit...89

Auto-suggestion...94

Reevaluation of values...100

On reading..139

On absolutes...150

Summary..156

Chapter 2: Meditation as a tool for development of mental discipline...158

Introduction..159

Basics of meditation...162

Basic meditation techniques...169

Advanced basic techniques..180

State of trance..187

Self-hypnosis...194

Archetypes..196
Effects of self-hypnosis based emotion control...................209
Inducing the state of trance without meditation...................216
Practical applications of self-hypnosis..............................220
The use of advanced meditation techniques.......................233
Asceticism..238
Summary..245
Chapter 3: Energy manipulation.......................................247
Introduction..248
Energy manipulation...258
Application of energy manipulation on emotion control.........270
Further explanation of the concept of energy manipulation.....280
Epilogue...285
Sources..289

Prologue

This book is written with beginners in mind. It teaches basics of philosophy and philosophic thought. Not as intended for the use in the academia, but rather for use in everyday life. It also teaches basic meditation techniques. It is assumed that the reader has no prior knowledge in any of these fields, so all the basic terms and concepts are explained with that premise in mind. This book explains primarily the basics with only essential mention of the advanced instructions. It sets up the foundation, or the framework of mental discipline. After mastering the basics advanced skill follows through training and experience as a matter of course, which makes this book useful for the people already familiar with these topics.

The primary goal of this work is to demonstrate how to develop mental discipline. The concept as understood here consists of controlling your own thoughts and emotions. The practice starts with basics of philosophy, primarily with Stoicism. It gives directions on shaping the suitable mentality, a mentality insensitive to harmful outside influences. In other words, mentality which promotes stoic indifference. Philosophy encourages rational, critical thinking instead of emotional thinking. As such it is very well suited to develop an objective, positive, and individualistic general attitude.

The second part of the practice consists of meditation exercises which further temper and build the mentality you develop through philosophy. They serve to improve your focus, stabilize your thoughts, and strengthen your willpower. Meditation exercises are the preparation for techniques used to control your emotions at will.

Achieving the goal of mental discipline will help you take control of your life to a higher degree, to shape your personality as you see fit, to conserve precious time and energy often trivially wasted, to adopt new useful habits, and to break harmful ones. This manual is based on authors own fourteen years of experience and experiments with meditation and various mental skills. There were many influences from diverse philosophical and religious systems. It represents only one of many approaches to the topic.

Concerning the control of emotions, there are two extremes: absence of emotions on the one side and complete lack of control on the other. By absence of emotions it is presumed not to be unable or unwilling to express them, but not having emotions, not reacting emotionally to the stimuli. Complete absence of emotions can be hard to maintain but it is not impossible to achieve. It is an interesting state to explore if induced willingly, or a problem that needs to be solved if it was caused by outside influences.

By having no control over emotions it is presumed being overly sensitive up to the point where in a more intense situation, a person is unable to function properly. Such people tend to exaggerate both good and bad in life, be it trivial or important. Dwelling on such events, especially on bad experiences is a terrible waste of time and energy. Effort spent on solving the problem at hand, self improvement, or everyday duties brings success instead of reinforcing it.

The control of thoughts aids greatly in the control of emotions, but its true benefit lies in general improvement of mental strength, concentration, willpower, and ability to filter out random, distracting thoughts. All of these factors bring general benefit because they increase your productivity in personal and professional life.

Becoming proficient in the two mentioned categories of mental discipline will help you realize there is more to it than that. Even though it contains some elements, this book is not an ethical, religious, or metaphysical system but a tool for unlocking personal potential that can be later used for further work of self-improvement. Almost anyone could find use for such knowledge, be they students, craftsmen, martial artists, business people etc. Whoever needs high concentration for their everyday work, wants to improve their efficiency and focus, or simply a way to deal with stress will find application for contents of this book.

Every action a person does, they do it with the help of their mind. Focused and trained mind will make every effort more effective. Whether you want to master your emotions and thoughts only to a degree that you can easily handle the pressure of modern life, or go further towards mastery of mind is a matter of personal choice and dedication.

Discipline and control do not imply emotional insensitivity, general indifference to others, absence of empathy, etc. but the ability to choose when to react and how intensely, and when to remain indifferent. When to think freely about whatever comes to your mind, and when to be focused on a single thought or action. Discipline and control imply freedom of thought, emotion, and action. It may seem that these techniques make life dull, depraved of any joy, but it is quite the opposite. They allow one to experience, enjoy, and appreciate life in a completely new way.

Chapter 1: Philosophy as basis for mental discipline

Introduction

Philosophy is the speculative science which studies entire reality by definition. It is divided into metaphysics, logic, epistemology, and ethics. Explaining these branches of philosophy in detail goes beyond scope of this book. Every one of them is as extensive as an individual science. But for the sake of completion and better understanding of philosophy in general, a very brief explanation is in order.

Metaphysics studies being as being and its attributes. It studies being in its entirety, not particular parts of being as natural sciences do.[1] In other words, metaphysics study principles that stand "behind" everything that exist, the laws that constitute the fabric of reality, those laws that make things exist. The laws that stand behind the laws of nature and laws of physics. Metaphysics differ between philosophical systems in which they are conceived as well as individual philosophers. The most famous metaphysics are Aristotle's and Plato's. Aristotle's metaphysics and philosophy had a major role in the entire western philosophy. It dominated philosophic thought through middle ages from Plotinus and Aurelius Augustine to Thomas Aquinas, and finally until Descartes and Kant. Far eastern religions have their own

1 Aristotle, *Metaphysics*, 1003a, 20-30

conception of the world, and thus their own metaphysics.

Metaphysics is a difficult concept to explain and it can be difficult to understand when encountered for the first time. Even though it is difficult to determine which metaphysics is the most truth like, it is still useful to be at least familiar with it because it helps in development of personal philosophy and understanding of religious or non religious systems of philosophy. It is also vital for every writer of fiction because it can make or break fantasy worlds.

Logic is the philosophic discipline that deals with proposition as its basic unit. Further it deals with consistency between connected propositions and inferences based on propositions. Logic in western philosophy was dominated by Aristotle's logic up until modern advances in the field. His series of works on logic are called Organon[2]. Form of logic that analyzes only propositions is called proposition logic. A classical example is:

Proposition 1 / premise: Socrates is a man.

Proposition 2 / premise: Men are mortal.

Inference / conclusion: Socrates is mortal.

It is very easy to determine consistency between simple propositions but it gets complicated in case of analyzing a longer

[2] https://plato.stanford.edu/entries/aristotle-logic/ (Aug. 27, 2019)

text or an argumentation on a certain subject. Another role of logic that helps with this problem is the study of rules of reasoning and argumentation. Errors in reasoning are called logical fallacies.

Predicate logic, considered a branch of mathematics, uses procedures similar to mathematics to express propositions or entire text in symbols, after which logical consistency is tested in manner similar to solving mathematical problems. It is used in programming, linguistics, engineering, and mathematics.

Critical thinking is the most basic form of logic which is of use to everyone. It is used simply by thinking about what you read or hear. Refrain from reacting or making a judgment by instinct before you determine what is it about and does it make sense.

Epistemology explores limits of human cognition and knowledge. It studies sources of knowledge and justification of belief, and the criteria of what makes a belief true, false, or justified. Knowledge is defined as justified true belief. For example, one knows that it is raining outside because he saw it through a window. He can also know if he was told by someone who does not usually lie. But if he did not perceive it in any way, or was told by someone unreliable, his belief would not be justified, and thus it could not be considered knowledge. This is just a brief, rough outline of epistemology. There are many views on the methodology and definition of knowledge in different systems of epistemology. More details can be found in the literature or online.[3]

Ethic is philosophic discipline that concerns itself with matters of proper behavior, or good and evil. It aims to define what way of life is the best for individuals and society in general, what kind of life brings lasting happiness. Ethic is the theory behind morality which is practical ethic or applied ethic. Ethics differ from system to system like other philosophic disciplines. There are many different approaches to the topic. The difference is mainly in the basis of ethical principles. The plurality of ethics is considered a good thing, while plurality of morals, or moral relativism, is considered negative. Moral relativism may occur when ethics and morality are considered one and the same. As various groups of people practice different ethics, there are various forms of morality as applied ethics. On the other hand, it can be argued that morality is not plural because it is a singular phenomena studied by plural ethical approach. Another argument for singular morality is to assume there is only one set of universal and true ethical/moral principles which must be discovered through ethics.

Examples of ethical basis: ancient Greek ethics of Plato and

---

3 https://plato.stanford.edu/entries/epistemology/#GET (Aug. 24, 2019)

Aristotle were equated with tradition, so the basis were values and religion of their society.

Natural law ethics are based on what is considered to be inalienable human right: self ownership, free will, and private property.

Kant based his ethics on duty, or what one ought to do in order to be moral.

Professional ethic establishes code of conduct in a given line of work, like medical ethics.

Religious ethics are based on religious teachings and metaphysics. Metaphysics may have an important role in ethics because it determines the worldview and hierarchy between beings. For example in Judeo-Christian tradition it is believed as it is written in Bible that humans are masters of the world, they are on top of hierarchy just under God, and all things living and non living exist to serve them.

This is where bioethics come into play as they study behavior of people towards nature and non-human animals.

Ethic as a philosophic discipline is also very useful for formation of personal philosophy because it deepens your perspective on the topic. Studying ethic as such will make you familiar with various problems and possible solutions that occurred throughout history of ethics, as well as help with understanding and analysis of related texts.

The importance of philosophy first and foremost lies in the promotion of critical thinking which is essential to develop a mindset necessary for self-improvement and development of self-discipline. The mindset of average people lacks dedication, objective self-criticism, and serious approach which causes them to give up easily on activities they consider too difficult. Serious approach, discipline, and motivation arise from ideals and goals. They can be formed with the help of philosophy.

The goal of philosophy is not in general skepticism in itself, but rather in refraining from judgment before you have enough facts to judge. Philosophy does not teach *what* to think, but *how* to think. As the meaning of the term "philosophy" (love for wisdom) suggests, its main goal is to search for knowledge, wisdom, and understanding, firstly for the sake of itself, as they say, and secondly for improvement of your life. Philosophic thinking changes perspective on what we experience in life, it gives an open mind receptive to new ideas. This is vital for development of a strong and healthy mentality. Everyone comes across a life-changing idea at some point in their life. It is stunning how a single useful idea, a change in mindset, can have a positive influence on your life. Many excellent ideas can be found in philosophy in general, and first philosophy described later in this book is Stoicism.

The Socratic approach can be considered a good basis for learning. The seemingly paradoxical saying attributed to Socrates is: "I know that I know nothing". How is it possible to say you know *nothing*, when you know at least that you know nothing? But that is not the point. The point is to acknowledge your own lack of knowledge, or in other words to realize that you know little, that you do not know everything. In the modern age of information this is apparent more than ever, yet people remain as biased as they ever were. The less they know, the more confident they get about their opinions. To properly learn new things, we must set aside what we think we know and approach with an open mind. Human memory and knowledge are not perfect. Even if you are well versed in a topic, it can be very useful to return to the basics, to renew what you learned before. Foreknowledge can help as much as it can hinder. It can help to interpret and understand new material, but it can also lead to misconceptions. For example, a student of western philosophy can find it easier to understand eastern philosophy because of their fundamental similarities. But the eastern philosophy deals with same problems in a different way, using a different way of expression which can cause confusion or misconceptions in a western educated philosopher.

Second important part of philosophy is the promotion of

abstract thinking. As a speculative science philosophy deals with many abstract ideas and concepts such as the purpose of human activity, limitations of human cognition, being, essence of being, metaphysical principles, ethical principles and values, as it was mentioned. As such it provides a different angle at which we observe and approach problems. It helps us to abstract ideas from material we encounter in everyday life, whether it is read from a book or experienced personally. It helps us to understand these ideas and to apply them. Without abstracting the essence of the material, we are unable to understand it and categorize it in our mind. This allows flexibility and creativity in application of knowledge. For that reason abstract thinking is vital foundation for learning.

Another important aspect of the study of philosophy is self knowledge. We must first know our self before we can properly understand the world and other people. *Gnoti seauton,* an ancient aphorism written at the entrance of the Oracle of Delphi. Self knowledge is the basis of all personal growth. How do you know yourself? What does it mean to know yourself? Is it not a question what could be called the question of all questions? There can be interpretations of the aphorism as there are people. And the problem is at least old as the spiritual pursuits of human race itself. What is a human being, what is human spirit, personality, consciousness, what is there in human mind, what is soul and does it exist? This is what many philosophers and psychologist tried to understand throughout history.

To put it a little more simply, a way to gain *some* self knowledge is to become honest to yourself. Practice introspection as objectively as possible and try to find your flaws and weaknesses. Find your true motivation among the winds of various wants, needs, instincts, and passions that pull you in different directions. It is easy to look at the positive, but it takes sincerity to admit the negative aspects of your personality to yourself. Do not hide or embellish them. Learn to be merciless towards yourself. Do not pay mind to what others think of you or what they say. They lie more often than not, to you and to themselves. Just like you do, just like we all do. Do not blame them for your failures. Do not use others as an excuse for your faults. In the vast majority of cases, people themselves are to blame for their own misfortune. Avoid any acts of pettiness, like holding grudges and vengefullness. They only chain you down in the mud of mediocrity. When people in your vicinity irritate you day after day and grate on your nerves, it is natural to be angry and, depending on the circumstances, to hate or despise them, to desire revenge. Your potential enemies want you to feel that way, they want you to make mistakes that will get you fired from work or even imprisoned. Do not give them this satisfaction. Let the hate and rage flow through you and use it to fuel your effort of self improvement. When your mind clears up from emotions, you will realize that revenge is nothing but emotional gratification, and this gratification will bring you no concrete benefit. However, as Nietzsche says: *"And if you are cursed at, I do not like it that you want to bless. Rather join a little in the cursing. And if you have been done a great wrong, then quickly add five little ones: a gruesome sight is a person single-mindedly obsessed by a wrong. [...] A small revenge is more human than no revenge"*[4] By all means, indulge in your revenge, if you will. After all if you do not fight back you will never have your peace. But know what revenge is, and keep in mind that a person who desires mental discipline needs a reason beyond emotional gratification. Find a healthy outlet for your negative emotions. As Marcus Aurelius advises in his Meditations, you can always rely on philosophy. Make your views clear, and when emotions cloud your judgment remind yourself about nature of things, as it is philosophic way.

This first chapter serves to explain the use of philosophy in general and to give ideas on how to develop a personal philosophy and ideals. Ideals are the basis for long therm self-improvement and mental discipline. In addition, the purpose of the first chapter is to encourage formation of an inquisitive mind

---

4 Nietzsche, F. 1954, *Thus Spoke Zarathustra,* Viking Press, New York, p. 179

which takes nothing for granted. By analyzing and trying to understand everything of interest we learn the most and gain the most wisdom. If the reader learns nothing else from this book but to question, it will still serve its purpose, because strong disagreement has inspired many a great mind to write their masterpieces.

An important part of mental discipline is the control of emotions. It is emphasized in this book because emotions can be as destructive as they can be productive for an individual. It is not as important to learn how to keep emotions at a minimal intensity as it is important to learn how to channel them towards something productive while limiting their potential damage. To be as productive and as successful as you can be, you must learn how not to dwell on negative emotions that arise from difficulty in life. Instead you should remain calm and focused, redirect your energy towards a more optimistic object. For example, self improvement and realizing your plans. Do not let the suffering break you. It is an unavoidable part of everyone's life. Do not avoid or run from suffering, because you will become complacent and weak. Face it head on to get stronger instead, in Nietzsche's terms, by surpassing the obstacle. Stoic and similar philosophies work well for this purpose, if they are implemented effectively. The first chapter of this book focuses on implementation of stoic philosophy and philosophy in general to achieve that goal among the others.

It is possible to use meditation techniques alone for controlling emotions, but without philosophical basis you may lack conviction and understanding necessary to develop mental discipline as seen in this book. Discipline is only a tool, without philosophy you lack wisdom to wield it effectively and productively. Philosophy serves to provide a framework of personal principles and ideals that motivate and give purpose to personal development, as it was mentioned before. If you do not see a purpose in your work and have no goal or ideal to strive for, you will rightfully feel your effort to be wasted. If your effort is for nothing, why persist in it? In addition, as Arnold Schwarzenegger said in his famous speech, if you have no goal you will wander around and you will achieve nothing significant. Without a goal your attention and effort will be dispersed between many interests and activities. It is important to have a goal, an idea of what you want to achieve in life and focus your effort towards it. His goal was to go to USA by reaching the top of body building. We too can strive towards any form of greatness ourselves. Well formed personal principles are not only useful for intellectual pursuit of knowledge, but they also serve as a basis for strong personality that will help you be happier and more successful in life.

Stoicism

Theory of Stoicism: basic concepts

It is hard to determine exact origin of emotion control techniques as it is for any other human activity. Some of the very first people who strove to control emotions were the Stoics. There were even older schools that had techniques for controlling one's own emotions, but Stoics are named first as their methods are the easiest to learn, based in philosophy, and can be used as a good basis for more complex techniques. To be disciplined means to be unmoved both on the outside and, more importantly, on the inside. The Stoics specialized in this form of mental discipline which makes their philosophy a very useful material for the purpose of this book. They were a group of ancient Greek philosophers whose ideal was to be unaffected by both good and bad of outside influences, and to live in harmony with nature.

For example, if someone close to you dies of natural causes, from the stoic point of view, you should not let it affect your everyday life because it is an inevitable natural occurrence that waits for us all. It is not wrong to mourn those who died, but death is a natural order of things which must be accepted. However, there is no purpose in pitying the dead because they are free from their earthly duties and suffering. Those who are left behind will feel the loss, and they mourn to accept the death of loved ones.

The contrary example is, if you are penniless and unexpectedly win the lottery, it is not something to be excited about, because excitement distracts you from your path and clouds judgment. Excitement or happiness themselves are not a problem in this case, but their potential damage is to be avoided by restraining your enthusiasm. With poor management of money you could quickly squander it and go back to zero. You might neglect your self improvement and turn to unrestrained self-destructive hedonism. In addition, fleeting happiness of such a fortunate turn of events does not necessarily lead to your permanent wellbeing, even more so if you squander the money as mentioned. According to Stoics, the true path in life is the life of virtue, life of wisdom, which leads to *eudaimonia,* or permanent bliss and happiness.

Stoicism formed over two thousand years ago, but it is still very useful and current. It will undoubtedly remain current for centuries to come. As long as people live in increasingly populated and complex societies, the need for Stoicism and similar philosophies will exist. Or better yet, as long as there is hardship and suffering Stoicism will be needed. The growth of society causes the increase of pressure in everyday life. People often feel lost and without purpose, especially if they do not know how to live in order to be fulfilled, or why to live in the first place. It is becoming harder and more exhausting to balance work, family, friends, and personal time. Traditional family model used to be a source of stability for people. Traditional gender roles used to give people an idea of what to do. They lived to support their family, especially men who were expected to fully provide for and protect it. Now this model is turned upside down by feminist and postmodern politics. But there is no point in reminiscing about "good" old times, because first of all they were not any better. Men slaved away to society, family, and government as much as they do today. The main difference is that they could derive some satisfaction from it, they could say they have a family and their efforts were not wasted. Today however, they may easily lose everything in divorce, both family and their property. They are without purpose more than ever. As a result, suicide rates are increasing. Many men use antidepressants and anti-anxiety drugs to deal with stress, while others use narcotics and alcohol. The situation is not much better for women. They certainly are better off at court of law, but they are equally unhappy and aimless as men. The feminist movement which supposedly has their best interest in mind is the main architecht of their misery.

Organized religion that was, and still is an important part of traditionalism provides no answers for the new generations.

Tradition was useful in times of its inception when it was means to pass on knowledge and ethics useful for survival of new generations. People did as their ancestors did and they did not knew any better. Organized religion as a part of tradition in pagan times was a reflection of how people perceived the world and their way of life. It was personified and mystified philosophy. Their gods and heroes were archetypes of everything they held dear and everything they feared. They were a reflection of people themselves. As religion evolved it turned more and more into politics and was perverted as a means of controlling the masses. Organized religion for the most part has nothing to do with spirituality but with politics. Churches in the West became "non-profit" political parties. All that remains from tradition is empty formality and celebrations void of deeper meaning. A tourist attraction at best, and brakes on intellectual progress at worst.

When tradition fails only philosophy can answer the existential questions. After all it is the only science that deals with such questions. Philosophy is highly underestimated in the world. Aimlessness, or lack of goal or purpose in life are some of the biggest problems that arise in the absence of philosophy. The problems that follow are anxiety and depression.

A lot of people could solve or alleviate these psychological problems simply by changing their way of thinking, their worldview. An individual can do nothing to change the political situation, but they can rebuild their own life. They can find a way of self-actualization outside modern politics. Outside societal expectations. Having a clear philosophic attitude will help you immeasurably to find a new meaning in life. To redefine your values and principles. With such a new mindset it is significantly easier to focus on your priorities, on things that really matter in life. It is easier to determine what is it that matters to you in the first place, and to break free from the mold of conformity to tradition and religion.

The way to start this change is to read classical works of philosophy. For example Plato's dialogues or *Meditations* by Marcus Aurelius. If one is interested in more details they can study Pre-Socratic period. Knowledge on metaphysics is useful for the study of religious texts. To start with that topic, besides Aristotle's book Metaphysics, studying early views on cosmology by Pre-Socratics can be a simpler introduction into that complex area.

With defiance to millennia old authorities comes additional stress of peer pressure. It is much more useful to focus on achieving your goals instead of burdening yourself with trivial matters like opinions, gossip, and problems of irrelevant people. Only the sense of achievement, the fact that you accomplished something significant with your own strength and effort may give you lasting satisfaction. But what is this significant accomplishment depends on personal preference. It is something that everyone must determine on their own. Some find their meaning in art, some in philosophy or natural science, some in perfecting a craft, some in martial arts, some in fitness, some in professional achievements; there can be as many goals as there are people. What matters the most is to choose something according to your talents and preference.

Stoics considered philosophy not simply a science, but a way of life[5]. This is another thing we can learn from them. In your philosophic activity you gain a new worldview, you learn about yourself and the world. In other words you notice things you would otherwise miss. You notice patterns of behavior, cause and effect, advantage and disadvantage. This is how people naturally learn, but with philosophy the process is deeper and more deliberate, more active than passive. If you learn new perspectives and ethical principles through reflection and philosophy, it would be reasonable to change your behavior accordingly to benefit from it. Would not your effort otherwise be a waste of time?

Only philosophy deals with concepts of purpose and meaning.

---

5   https://plato.stanford.edu/entries/stoicism/#Phil (Mar. 20, 2019)

Only through philosophy can we determine and decide the purpose and the goal of every human activity. Philosophy was not only the first science, but it is also the queen of all forms of science because it makes their purpose known. Yet in modern day, in the western society even its status as a science is being denied. One may argue that you do not need philosophy to decide purpose or meaning for anything, that scientific practice, of computer science for example, can determine its own meaning. But the act of thinking about purpose of something is inevitably philosophic activity, just like act of calculation is inevitably mathematical activity; regardless of it being used to count money, birds in a tree, or to determine the carrying capacity of a bridge in civil engineering. Think about the purpose of your everyday activities to gain the most benefit from them. Align your hobbies with your goals and aspirations by choosing those that will inspire creativity and effort.

The stoic school of philosophy was founded by Zeno of Citium in 3rd century BCE. Similarly to other Hellenistic philosophers and schools of thought, not many Stoic books were preserved. Only those from the last, Roman period of Stoicism remain complete, written by Seneca, Epictetus, and Marcus Aurelius. Only fragments quoted and commented in works of other philosophers remain from the books written by the three first heads of Stoicism: Zeno of Citium, Cleanthes, and Chrysippus.[6] As mentioned before, part of stoic ethics was to live in harmony with nature. For ancient Greeks that meant to live in accordance with the divine law, called Logos, which was also considered as the law of Nature in general.

Obviously, divine Logos has a religious side to it. Similarly to notions present in Judeo-Christian tradition, it can be interpreted as surrendering to God's will or fate. Aligning your will with the will of God, or the will of Zeus in Stoic terms. Difficulty in life could be seen as a test of faith or divine punishment. If everything is planned and occurs as willed by god(s) what else is there but to endure and live on? It was not unusual at that time for schools of philosophy to have some religious elements. Marcus Aurelius described life as devotion to one's duties, honoring gods, and philosophic contemplation. Such a lifestyle certainly has a religious element, but we can find something non-religious to learn from it: dedication to your goals and philosophic contemplation. Besides Stoics, other schools like Cyrenaics, Epicureans, Pythagorean school, Platonic Academy, Aristotle's Peripatetic school, etc. all had their own way of life which had some resemblance to religion. This is not unusual considering that philosophy represented a way of life to contemporary philosophers, so naturally they lived according to their ideology.

6   https://plato.stanford.edu/entries/stoicism/#Source (Mar. 19, 2019)

Average people who live more according to instinct and emotion rather than according to reason, will inevitably consider any form of structure, rules, and principles in life to be a religious or religion-like element. They will consider it foolish and useless because it demands action and change. Because it gets in the way of their conformist, mediocre, easy-going lifestyle.

The main difference between philosophic and religious worldview is in the fact that the former is subject to change, while the latter is fixed and resists change. Philosophy seeks the truth while religion prescribes the truth. Philosophy questions dogma while religion is based on it. Similarly to Greek schools of philosophy, eastern religions/philosophies, like Buddhism and Taoism for example, are primarily a philosophic way of life with religious elements. They are not a *revealed* religion, but a result of generations of human effort. As such they are more likely to evolve than revealed religions. Religious elements of ancient philosophy, however, are more important for history of philosophy than for application of Stoic wisdom. The supposed will of god(s) is not reason enough to accept something as a fact, to accept events as they are, or to accept a specific way of life. A philosopher needs to find answers to existential questions for himself, regardless of existence of divinity. He must use his own strength of mind in order to find out the truth and the purpose in life. To define his ethical values and principles.

Stoics considered humans to be rational animals, so as part of their nature they were expected to live in accordance with reason. As rational animals, humans were the only ones to know the laws of nature to which they were to submit.[7] To defy the laws of nature was considered a futile effort. Instead, according to Stoics, humans should have changed their inner state and indifferently accepted their fate. To be able to achieve this level of indifference was not considered an easy task by Stoics. On the contrary, to become indifferent to difficulties a person should have gained sufficient wisdom and understanding of life and Logos through intense self-discipline and philosophic reflection.

Fate, reason, and Nature are fundamental concepts of Stoic philosophy. Nature is not only Earth, but also the entire universe, or cosmos in general. According to Stoics and contemporary Greek religion, Cosmos is made by the gods from unorganized matter, from Chaos into Order (Cosmos). Everything that exist and occurs in Nature is necessary and natural. New things, new beings, are made from matter, and when they die, or are destroyed, they are reduced to their original state of matter. This matter is then used to form new beings. This constitutes the cycle of life, destruction, and formation of new beings. The cycle is

---

[7] Copleston, F., 1993, *A History of Philosophy Vol. 1,* Image Books, New York, 395 p.

governed by Divine law, or Law of Nature, or Logos, they are all the same thing. Everything happens according to divine providence and Law which constitute Fate. Everything that happens to man, his fate, is predetermined by the gods. Going against one's fate and nature causes only suffering. While living according to nature and resigning to fate brings wellbeing and alleviates suffering.

The next important part is the nature of an individual, or a being in general. The nature of a being is the same as its essence, or that which demonstrates its way of being, the way it exists,what are its attributes and properties, or what it is in the most general terms: human, rock, dog, tree, etc.. Essence is philosophic *terminus technicus*. More details on its definition can be found in books on metaphysics or online.[8] Beings differ from one another by their nature. They are what they are and their nature cannot be changed. You can identify as a helicopter as much as you want, but you will never be a helicopter, but what you were born to be, what you are by nature: a human, male or female.

For example, in Aristotelian terms: a rock is inanimate by nature, it has volume, mass, color, etc.; a plant has all that, but can also grow and reproduce; an animal has all these properties of a

---

8   https://plato.stanford.edu/entries/aristotle-metaphysics/#SubsEsse (Nov. 29, 2019)

plant, but can also move in space; a human along with mentioned properties of other beings also has reason by nature. Reason allows humans to understand their nature, nature of other beings, and natural law. Unlike humans who are able to choose how to act, other animals are constrained by their nature to live according to their instinct. This part of anthropology was shared by Aristotle, Plato, Stoics, and later even by Christian philosophers among others. Expressed in these simple terms or in a different way, we can know for fact that humans are different form other beings and that they behave in certain way by observing reality. It is true that many animals are intelligent. They learn and adapt to their surroundings. Many can even use tools. But no animal other than man demonstrates the level of intellect capable of developing technology and culture, or possesses creativity capable of producing art. No other animal is capable of human level of senseless cruelty.

While it is true that humans stand above other animals due to reason, it is also true that humans are influenced by their subconscious instincts, emotions, and urges to a shocking degree. This is probably the main reason for human imperfection. Some went so far as to question the existence of free will, like Nietzsche. People do many self destructive things just because they feel good. The strongest human instincts are survival and reproduction. When either is in danger people are capable of all kinds of irrational and violent acts. The only way to fight irrationality is through knowledge and training of self-discipline. To fight emotions means to give up on many pleasures they offer. To which degree is this possible depends on the training and human limitations.

To act according to one's nature, in the context of Stoicism, it means to act according to reason. Reason is limited by emotions, instincts, and desires. The task of a philosopher is to free his reason from these influences through study and use of philosophy. Humans are a part of the whole called Nature, or world. In stoic terms, it is reasonable to live in harmony with Nature. This means, as Marcus Aurelius asserts throughout *Meditations*, to accept your fate without resistance, to focus on your duties, and live in harmony with other people and society in general. To be indifferent does not mean to stubbornly ignore what is going on around you. On the contrary. It means to actively observe in order to understand everything that is. To see clearly things and events for what they are, their cause and effect[9]. But to remain emotionally unaffected before outside influences. This is where reason comes into play. It is hard to stress enough the importance of reason in stoic philosophy. When you are able to notice and

9   Aurelius, M., 2003, Meditations, Modern Library, New York, book 3, par. 11

understand cause and effect of everything that happens to you, according to Stoics, you will know that it is futile to resist your fate and find your inner peace. In different words, when you realize it is pointless to get upset when things do not go your way, you will find inner peace.

According to Stoics, in order to be happy one must align his actions according to reason. To do this, he must ignore his emotions and instincts that pull him away from reason, which is divine and spiritual, towards bodily, earthly, and carnal. Stoics did not despise the carnal or propose severe asceticism. They proposed moderation instead of blind indulgence of vice. Many Greek philosophers considered mind/reason to be the characteristic which makes humans similar to gods because it gave them godlike creativity and understanding. As mentioned before, reason allows humans to understand the Law of Nature. Therefore, living according to reason is living according to Nature. This briefly explains three fundamental concepts of stoic philosophy.

Theory of Stoicism: ethics

According to Stoics, only life in accordance with reason is virtuous life, and only virtuous life brings happiness. The pursuit of *cudaimonia*[10] through ethical way of life was one of the main goals of ancient Greek philosophy. It is not wrong to say that people strive for that same goal even today, philosophers or not. Who does not wish to be happy? But, philosophic pursuit of this goal is not as simple as that. It requires a precise definition of what is it that brings happiness. What kind of lifestyle will make us happy? Is happiness a goal in itself, or just a positive byproduct of a quality lifestyle? And what is happiness in the first place? There can be as many definitions of happiness as there are people, and that activity which makes it clear and easier to determine what is it that will bring us happiness is philosophy. Specific part of philosophy concerned with the way of life is ethics. Philosophy in general allows us to organize our thoughts on abstract and complex matters, while ethics as a specific philosophic discipline deals with behavior and lifestyle. It helps us define our values, to align our way of life with a specific goal, to distinguish between advantages and disadvantages in everyday life. It is easy to lose sight of your goals and fall into self destructive decadence of modern life. Decadence is not necessarily what is seen in religion or traditional society of older times, but whatever distracts you from maintaining your wellbeing and your higher goals can be considered decadence and

---

10   The term refers to the concept of lasting happiness and fulfillment present in ancient Greek philosophy

deprivation. Leisure is also necessary for that purpose, to get rid of fatigue and stress, to recharge your strength for a new effort. But too much leisure is counterproductive because it squanders your potential.

Philosophers of ancient times wanted to define principles and virtue necessary for proper life. This is something that even we today must do for ourselves if we want to to have order and discipline which gives meaning and wellbeing in life. In modern days, stoic notions of divine law and immutable, merciless fate are of little importance. The other notion of living in accordance to reason, however, is a matter that should be looked upon more closely.

In stoic ethics it is considered to be good anything that contributes to perfection of a being according to its nature, namely virtue. Virtue unconditionally and necessarily contributes to happiness.[11] In Plato's dialogues this is taken as a given. It is not always satisfyingly demonstrated why virtue is always useful. Bad, or evil, is everything that contributes to misery of a being, namely vice. Vice is a corruption of reason. Things that are nether useful nor harmful by themselves, but depending on their use, are

---

11   https://www.iep.utm.edu/stoiceth/#H3 (April, 28, 2019)

considered "indifferents" by Stoics.[12]

Passions are defined by Stoics as a disobedience of judgment to reason, an irrational excessive movement of the soul. Since reason is integral part of human nature, irrationality is an unnatural state. The four general types of passion are distress, fear, appetite, and pleasure. Pleasure and fear are caused by present object, while appetite and distress are caused by future object. Corresponding good states are joy, caused by present object, and wish and caution both caused by future object. For example, a virtuous person feels joy in presence of a friend, wishes to see a friend if possible, but has no negative thoughts or feelings when separated from the friend. Virtuous person is cautious of future danger, but does not fear it. A vicious person is a slave to their passions. They blindly indulge in pleasures and suffer when pleasure is unavailable.[13] It is important to take in consideration that *"virtuous person is not passionless in the sense of being unfeeling like a statue. Rather, he mindfully distinguishes what makes a difference to his happiness—virtue and vice—from what does not. This firm and consistent understanding keeps the ups and downs of his life from spinning into the psychic disturbances or "pathologies" the Stoics understood passions to be."*[14] This explains Stoic conception of passion well and brings out one of the points of stoic indifference: to control passions so

---

12 Ibid.
13 Ibid.
14 Ibid.

they do not control you.

Indifferents are subdivided into preferred and dispreferred subcategories. Examples of preferred indifferents are life, health, pleasure, beauty, strength, wealth, good reputation, and noble birth. Examples of dispreferred indifferents are death, disease, pain, ugliness, weakness, poverty, low repute, and ignoble birth.[15] With Stoic ethics taken into consideration, these characteristics are not a necessary requirement for a virtuous life, but they contribute to inner peace positively or negatively respectfully. Most people would consider them a form of good or evil, but they do not fit the definition of good and evil. If one is ugly, sickly, and in pain, for example, these attributes may negatively affect their inner peace, but their virtue will not suffer if they maintain proper attitude. It does not matter if they do not use it as an excuse for indulging in vice.

The most appreciated virtues in stoic ethics were wisdom, justice, courage, and moderation. They were traditional Greek values/virtues, also inherited from Plato who discussed the same virtues in his *Republic,* while Aristotle discussed the topic in his *Nicomachean Ethics.*

Justice is a virtue mostly relevant in relation to other people. In Plato's *Republic* it is defined as every member of city-state doing

15 Ibid.

what suits them best by nature[16], or on individual level, every part of the soul (reason, spirit, and appetite) doing its own function. Marcus Aurelius defined it as being tolerant[17] and treating everyone equally. Self discipline deals primarily with attitude towards self, so only part of justice as defined we can use, is to be polite to strangers and people who treat us well, to refrain from argumentative behavior, and to tolerate different opinion.

Courage is a virtue important in all ages. To be courageous is to face difficulty instead of running away. It is to dare living according to your principles when its hard and when it makes you stand off from the masses, despite fear and danger. To face your flaws and failures while honestly recognizing your mistakes. For Stoics, courage is to calmly accept your fate, to keep your inner peace despite suffering and difficulty in life. Plato defines it as an ability to protect in any way, or a proper opinion on what is frightening and what is not frightening. This ability is gained, according to Plato, through suitable education.[18] From experience we can say he was right, at least partially. Brave people fear only real danger and are able to function under stress. Cowardly people do not have a realistic idea of what is frightening, so they fear discomfort, change, and trivial matters all the time. For example, fear of losing loved ones, or that something bad may happen to

16   Plato, *Republic*, 433 a
17   Aurelius M., 2003, *Meditations*, Modern Library, New York, book 4, par. 3
18   Plato, *Republic*, 429 c – 430 c

them. Something bad can happen at any time to anyone. If there is no direct perceivable threat from anything or anyone, what is there to fear? They fear and overreact even when learning of a past danger. For example, if a car passes by you at high speed just as you stepped on the road. Nothing happened and there is no more danger, you may be startled for a second, but what is there to fear any more? If your nerves are strained like this all the time, you will not be able to function under stress of a real danger. There is a thin line, however, between bravery and foolishness. Provoking random people because of difference in opinion can easily get you killed. Provoking protected political groups in public can get you in prison. Is it brave, is it worth your health and freedom to speak the truth to the deaf?

Moderation can be defined as proper choice. Plato in *Republic*[19] defines it as a form of harmony between desires. A moderate man is, as contemporary proverb said, "stronger than himself". This means he is able to refrain from acting upon his impulses, to indulge his desires in a constructive and healthy manner. To be moderate is to indulge in pleasures with good measure where most people cannot restrain themselves. To balance work and recreation in a productive and healthy manner. Passions, desires, emotions, and instincts are moderate as long as they remain within rational limits. If they become too intense,

19 Plato, *Republic*, 430 d – 432 a

they are irrational and harmful to the individual. For example, if someone is experiencing intense hatred, anger, sorrow, lust, etc, he loses objective view on the situation.

Wisdom can be defined as a combination of theoretical knowledge and experience. It was mainly defined as factual knowledge by Aristotle and Plato. Socrates included intellectual honesty and humility as part of wisdom.[20] Humility itself may not be a requirement for wisdom, but it can be a sign of wisdom. Dumb people tend to be overconfident, overbearing, and arrogant. Intelligent people can be like that too, but such behavior does not befit a wise man. Calm and polite attitude will get you much further in life than arrogant and entitled behavior. But neither excessive humility of just taking insults, taunts, and mocking does befit a wise man. As the expression goes, even Buddha will strike back if you hit him three times. There is no singular answer for every situation, therefore it takes wisdom to determine the best course of action.

From everyday life we can see that having factual knowledge or being intelligent is not enough to be wise. Many intelligent and highly educated people can produce great results in science, for example, but are clueless in business or interacting with other people. Thus they get easily exploited by people of lesser intelligence, but of higher skill in social interactions. To be wise it

20 https://plato.stanford.edu/entries/wisdom/#WisKno (April, 16, 2019)

is important to use philosophic reflection to unify factual knowledge into a whole. With wisdom, one should be able to understand cause and effect, end goal and purpose, advantage and disadvantage in every situation. They should be able to make the best possible decision when facing a problem. It is hard to make decisions without knowing all the facts, but experience and trained intuition will help fill in the gaps. This is what we could call wisdom.

Philosophers in Hellenistic period considered philosophy to be the most important theoretical knowledge. At the beginning philosophy encompassed most of the available knowledge in their society. It reached from grammar and art to metaphysics, physics, biology, and medicine. Different philosophers focused on different fields of knowledge. As the total sum of knowledge increased, individual sciences divided from philosophy developing through centuries to what we have today. Depending on their philosophy and worldview ancient philosophers developed different ethics which prescribed different ways to achieve a blissful life. Understanding and intuition that stem from wisdom, which is the knowledge and experience on how the world functions as a whole, allow you to lead a more fulfilling life. In more concrete terms, with wisdom you have higher understanding of laws and disciplines that govern the society, such as economics, politics, behavior of people, business, religion, philosophy, etc. Wisdom, as defined formerly, implies that an individual must study and understand these mentioned areas knowledge in order to be wise. A wise person will not be distracted by trivial matters and misinformation they encounter in everyday life. In stoic terms, they will be unaffected by irrelevant and unchangeable facts so they can focus on what is important and achievable, and thus lead a happier life.

For example, as an individual you cannot change political and economical situation of the country you live in, but you can adapt and make the best you can within the given circumstances. This is what means not to be distracted by unchangeable facts. You could lament your circumstances or engage in political activism, which is futile for the most part, or focus your time and energy on managing your assets and self improvement to ensure your wellbeing. Complain less and focus on bad aspects of life less, but think more about what you can do to improve your life.

Understanding in this context could be defined as internalization and appreciation of concepts, principles, and values. It is a mental comprehension which, in stoic terms, changes or stabilizes the inner state. It allows true indifference as a stoic goal. The primary obstacles towards this goal are dishonesty towards self, interpersonal relations which cause negative emotions, and the inefficient control of emotions in general. Addressing these problems is one of the main goals of this book.

Application of Stoicism

It cannot be said that Stoics really used such techniques as they are described in this book. These techniques are inspired by, or at least in the spirit of Stoicism because they are based on philosophical thinking and rationalization. In essence, the effectiveness of stoic philosophy lies in changing your mentality, in accepting events in life as they are, indifferently and dispassionately so that you can freely choose the best course of action.

If we want to use Stoicism in modern day, it is necessary to remove the archaic and redundant parts. However, there is a limit to how far we can go in this intention. If we remove too much of stoic ethics we will be left only with superficial notions, something like a Stoic fortune cookie. We can safely remove religious influences and the concept of Fate. While developing personal philosophy and ethics, it is intellectually lazy to rely on answers already formed by religion. There can be some influences if one is religious, but too much influence will only make it a variation of existing religious philosophy. It is the philosophic way to rely on your own effort, reason, and reflection to form a worldview, to reevaluate your beliefs. Only by using reason alone can we reach a universal ethics. In addition, you can be sure the chosen philosophy or a worldview suits you only if you shape it by yourself, for yourself.

Concerning the concept of Fate, if we assume that everything is predetermined, why invest effort in self improvement? Why work hard to ensure your wellbeing in the future? If this was the case, no matter what you do in life, you would still end up successful or unsuccessful depending on your fate. But we know from experience and from biographies of exceptional people, that success is achieved for the most part by effort and wisdom. On the previous example of winning the lottery, if you manage your new capital wisely you can invest and earn much more thus becoming successful. On the other hand you can be unwise by spending all the money irrationally and going back to zero. To become successful without such a streak of luck takes even more wisdom and effort. However, there is something we can learn from the Stoic concept of Fate. We must face unexpected difficulty with rational indifference. Even though unexpected problems can be reduced by developing a set of useful skills and efficient asset management, if you panic in the face of danger there is little you can do regardless of how prepared you may be.

An aspect of Stoic indifference and the concept of fate is: that which *is* and cannot be changed should be accepted as such. If it is not possible to realize your intention or a certain ideal you should accept it and move on. It is a waste of energy to dwell upon it. People are often unhappy with their body, appearance, social status, health, etc. and some of those things cannot be changed. They dwell on it for years, leading themselves to despair and reinforcing the problem in their mind. In the process they make it much worse than it actually is. In such situations one must make peace with themselves and accept the fact at hand, because it cannot be changed. Once accepted the problem will not be such a burden, and in some cases will cease to exist.

In addition to mentioned factors, the political and economic state of the country in which one lives do not change easily as well. This is another fact that must be accepted as such. There is no point in lamenting the unfavorable conditions, but you should try to find a way to thrive despite the difficulty. If there is nothing that can be done, you can always move to a more suitable environment. Adapt or perish - that is the law of nature and economy.

If the matter at hand is something that *can* be changed, one should focus on a way to change it rather than dwelling on the fact that it is. This is what people fail to implement when they are unhappy with something in their life.

In terms of developing discipline, Stoic ethics has an advantage over Aristotle's or Plato's ethics. The latter developed their ethics primarily with functionality and wellbeing of *polis* in mind. An individual was of secondary concern. He was just a member of *polis* who was expected to play his role for the good of the community according to its ethical principles. Their ethics certainly has merit in defining basic terms and specific virtues, as demonstrated before. Stoic ethics, even though it shares a lot with Aristotle and Plato, has an individualistic approach. It aims to help an individual to reach inner peace for sake of himself first, and for the sake of society second. As such, their ethics contains advice on developing mentality that can be considered a part of mental discipline. Mentality or attitude is the concept of primary concern for development of discipline aimed in this book. The attitude cannot be described accurately in words, but it can be shown with example and theory. It can be understood and learned through experience and reflection.

Rational thought and inner calm pursued by Stoics are a useful and a universal goal. It is achieved by controlling your thoughts and emotions. We can learn about self control by observing and adopting some of the Stoic principles and advice. They can serve as reminder, a direction in which we can guide our way of thinking. As you reflect on Stoic aphorisms found in this, or in

Stoic books try to determine which ones are of use to you, which ones are outdated, and which ones do not refer to you. There can be interpretations other than those that have been originally intended. Use your creativity to extend their point of view to your benefit.

It is useful to have a certain idea of what you want to become in the end. Stoics had an archetype, or an ideal of the Sage they strove for which can be of use even now. An ideal like this unifies stoic ethics in a more substantial form which we can emulate at the beginning. It is an example of a goal that focuses your energy in a single direction. As your self development progresses you surpass the need for these auxiliary tools. If we want to successfully change our mentality by using this method, we must take Stoic philosophy seriously with an intention of using it. Otherwise Stoic principles and advice will be just empty words to us.

The Sage represented the pinnacle of philosophic pursuit and wisdom for the Stoics. He is the one who achieved their ideal of virtue and indifference. Marcus Aurelius can be considered a good example of a Sage. This is shown by his thoughts and ethics described in his diary/book Meditations. He was the most powerful man in the world who could have had anything he wanted. Yet he chose a simple, moderate, borderline ascetic lifestyle. This demonstrates his willpower and ideals. He firmly believed that modest life is better than life of extravagance and carnal pleasures, which helped him to resist temptation. It does not require an inhuman effort to live according to similar ethics as he did. Like every exceptional lifestyle, it just requires a goal (ideal), a routine (habit), and a healthy dose of self discipline. Another good aspect of Aurelius' philosophy is that it is simple. Similar viewpoints can be reached by reflection and common sense. Which means that someone with little or no knowledge of Stoic philosophy can reach similar perspective if they think about the same topics.

When observing a lifestyle of an exceptional person, it is important to keep in mind that they have developed their routines and habits according to *their* biorhythm, duties, needs, wants, and abilities. If we want to learn from them and achieve something similar, we cannot just do as they did. A simple example is fitness routine. People who follow other people's training regime give up quickly because they do not have the required fitness level or discipline developed through long term effort. We certainly can learn from others and adopt some elements that are suitable for us. Specifically, ideas and concepts that guide and inspire our effort. It is very important to slowly develop your own abilities and habits to become successful in your intention. To develop a personal philosophy or discipline similar to a Stoic Sage, we must start with the basics while keeping the ideal in mind.

What does the archetype of Sage represent for this book? It can already be guessed based on what was said in the theory of Stoicism. The unexpressed image can be equally useful as a precisely defined concept. The archetype of Sage offers many elements that one can choose to follow. When we imagine a Sage, we imagine someone calm, wise, rational, and old. The primary focus of this book is self control and discipline. It does not mean superficial control in the sense of enduring negative emotions without acting upon them, but in the sense of controlling emotions themselves. It means to control their intensity and their formation. It is not healthy to endure negative emotions without release. They must be shaped and directed at will, or destroyed at will when they are no longer needed. The first part of control is the control of thoughts learned through study of philosophy and refined through meditation described in the next chapter of this book. Second part is using your willpower to directly control emotions which will be covered in the final chapter.

Wisdom is another virtue acquired through study in general and the study of philosophy in particular. It was previously defined as a combination of experience and theoretical knowledge. In a general sense wisdom represents intuition and good judgment that make it easier to realize your plans in society. In a more restricted sense, it represents self knowledge. It is an easily underestimated concept. A person has direct insight into their physical and mental state, so they think they know all there is to know about themselves. "I am *I*. I feel what I feel." Thus it seems that there is nothing else to know besides that. But we know by experience that people often overestimate or underestimate themselves. They are unsure about their motivation and the reason why they feel the way they do. They are either not confident in their abilities or overconfident. Wisdom or self knowledge as intended here is developed by experience through objective observation of emotions and thoughts, self discipline in private life, and putting your skills to the test in everyday interaction with other people. It is very easy to remain calm when alone, but it takes skill to be indifferent when faced with irritating people, or difficult problems. To objectively look at emotions means to observe them with your mind. To observe how they form and how they affect your behavior without any following emotions like anger or guilt. It means to acknowledge your emotions and urges as they are, without embellishment. To acknowledge both your good sides and your flaws, faults, and weaknesses for sake of self improvement. This cold introspective observation is the skill that allows you to choose your mental attitude when the situation requires it. In addition it helps you recognize the mechanism to control emotions with willpower in later stages of training.

Last element of the Sage archetype that can be highlighted here is indifference. As it was already mentioned, it is closely related to wisdom. When a person is wise/knowledgeable, he will not be easily surprised or angered by lifestyle or behavior of other people. In addition to wisdom, indifference is also related to discipline. With training thoughts and emotions do not run wild, so it is not as easy to provoke an emotional response from a disciplined individual. Thus, indifference means to be emotionally uninvolved with things that are not important or interesting to you. In other words, you simply do not care about irrelevant things. It is a passive state of mind gained through training. In these terms indifference could also be defined as the art of not caring, or at least selective caring. One of the most important things in life is to learn how not to care about irrelevant things. What will be considered important and interesting depends on your priorities, values, and personal philosophy. When you are truly indifferent you do not get upset by anything. You can get angry all you want if things do not go your way, but it will not solve your problems, it will not undo your cause of distress. So what is the point of getting angry? When you understand and internalize this Stoic point of view, it is only natural to be indifferent. Indifference does not mean you should just accept your situation and do nothing to change it. It means you should be emotionally unaffected, but not inactive. You should not be helplessly overwhelmed by a problem, but calmly accept it as it is so that you can solve it efficiently.

The Stoic inspired way of developing before mentioned control of thoughts is rationalization. In this context, to rationalize does not mean to justify or to find an excuse, but to understand and to find the reasoning and the cause behind actions of self and others. It means to analyze rationally and logically, to observe things from different perspective. To determine gains and losses, advantages and disadvantages. Rationalization must become a habit. The habit can be developed by rationalizing not only philosophic views, but also everyday events and behavior of people that influence us. The main goal of rationalization is to change from impulsive emotional judgment towards logical and rational judgment. Emotional thinking is an instinct, and when we lack information to form a judgment we use our bias to fill in the gaps. It is a philosophic way to refrain from judgment when we do not have all the facts, and it is wise to speculate logically and rationally if we must judge in this case. To judge on what is the most probable, not on what we fear or want to be the truth. Through rationalization we strive to distinguish with a cool head

53

what is important from what is irrelevant. When you calmly observe something that bothers you, you will often realize it is not worth your attention. For example, conversations with people who annoy you. Whatever they say or do to bother you, it does not really matter. You have your own life and your own problems, so why bother with theirs? This realization can be compared to the moment when you suddenly understand something you have been trying to figure out, or when you suddenly get a good idea. When it is fully accepted into your mind it will cause a significant change in your emotions. Trough these moments of clarity you gradually shape your mentality towards Stoic indifference, or other preferences.

Instinct can be at least reduced, if not removed by habit. To make a substantial change in your mentality, gradually change your usual thought patterns. Regularly reflect on your emotional state, actions and reactions. Try to find the causal train of thoughts that leads to irrational choices and gradually change it towards something more productive. Avoid dwelling on your problems and events that cause you emotional distress. Think about how to solve these problems and what to do to improve yourself instead. Reflect on opinions that form your worldview, and on philosophic principles that you may hold or may have read about. Strive to think in logical, rational, and emotionally neutral terms. Do not think about how things make you *feel* but what is the *real state* of things. Once this way of thinking becomes a habit, you will have taken a step towards higher mental discipline. It will improve your introspection and help to recognize your strengths and weaknesses.

Rationalization does not restrict your freedom of thought, it just changes your perspective. Perspective is very important because, as the famous Milton's quote says: "mind can make heaven out of hell and hell out of heaven". Human mind is very powerful. Your subjective reality, or the way you feel, or your general attitude towards self and the world, dictates your perception. It influences your thought patterns, your goals and aspirations, your emotions and desires. In order to be happy and successful, positive outlook on life is imperative. With defeatist attitude you will see nothing but obstacles in your way, and these obstacles will be an excuse to give up. Obstacles are to be surpassed in order to become stronger. And where one person sees an obstacle, another sees opportunity. This is the difference in perspective. Stoic philosophy is all about perspective, which will be demonstrated next.

Stoic advice and aphorisms

"Let it happen, if it wants, to whatever it can happen to. And what's affected can complain about it if it wants. It doesn't hurt me unless I interpret its happening as harmful to me. I can choose not to."[21]

"Choose not to be harmed—and you won't feel harmed. Don't feel harmed —and you haven't been."[22] – **You will be offended if you choose to be.**

These quotes express the essence of stoic philosophy. The way we see reality highly depends on our attitude. We will be broken by misfortune if we let it break us. We will not be offended if we take no offense. We get angry or offended by instinct and by habit. We must strive to break this habit and develop an insensitive mentality.

"To be like the rock that the waves keep crashing over. It stands unmoved and the raging of the sea falls still around it. —It's unfortunate that this has happened. No. It's fortunate that this has happened and I've remained unharmed by it—not shattered by the present or frightened of the future. It could have happened to anyone. But not everyone could have remained unharmed by it"[23] – **Remain calm in face of difficulty.**

Similarly to the first quote, this one also expresses well the stoic concept of indifference. Be brave and stand tall. Do not let

---

21 Aurelius, M., 2003, *Meditations*, Modern Library, New York, book 7, par. 14
22 Ibid. book 4, par 7
23 Ibid. book 4, par 49

anything break you. Do not let your will weaken, keep it strong. Misfortune can befall anyone, you must remain strong and calm to solve your problems, or to endure personal tragedy.

Stoically firm and indifferent mentality as described previously is one of the goals of this book. It can be defined as a state of high level of self control, discipline, and concentration. In summary, this is achieved by exercise which gradually forms a habit, as mentioned. The habit which needs to be formed is to primarily think about matters important for self improvement on personal and professional level. Secondarily, it is important to avoid thinking about things that distract you from self improvement. That way you are concentrated on your goal which makes it easier to ignore everything else, especially trivial matters. This becomes natural when you spend a lot of time training mentally and physically. Everything else that does not contribute enough to your pursuit of greater ability and personal and/or professional accomplishment will feel like a waste of time.

The first step to achieve the stoic calm is to determine what is it that bothers you the most and why. Analyze with a cool head everyday situations in which you react intensely. If you are unable to think during the event, think about it when you regain your composure. Once you determine what are the causes of your negative reactions, whether it be bad temper or feeling offended, you can start working on fixing the problem. Next step is to break the habit of reacting intensely and form the habit of restraint. If you refrain from reacting on the stimuli immediately, you get an opening to think briefly about your next step. That way you break the habit. It becomes easier to control yourself and to avoid being controlled by others. Once the problem is understood through the described practice it is much easier to fix it. In some cases the problem may cease to exist.

Temperance or moderation is the virtue that helps guide and shape habit. The essence of moderation, defined before as proper choice, is in avoiding the extremes on both ends. Excess in the broadest sense of the term leads to mental and physical weakness. Moderation emphasizes quality over quantity. For example, too much or too little exercise damages the body. It is the same with too much or too little food and drink. Only optimal exercise and nourishment promote health. If we indulge too much in things we like, the pleasure we draw from them gradually weakens. The required amount of stimulation grows so we end up, in opium addict terms, "chasing the dragon". Even from hedonistic point of view, it is not useful to overindulge, but to enjoy with good measure in order to maximize the benefit, the pleasure. Uncontrolled excessive urges and emotions lead to laziness, procrastination, gluttony, and similar flaws which cause problems in health, social and professional life. In the extreme case personal flaws can lead to crime like assault, theft, murder, and rape. All of them caused by uncontrolled urges like anger, hatred, greed, and lust. Some people get to a state of extreme laziness and obesity. They lack the slightest willpower to get out of the bed, let alone break the routine that led them to such degeneracy.

In milder terms, uncontrolled wants and needs lead to waste of time and resources. In fact, time itself is the most scarce resource of all. It can only be spent and never earned back. That is why we must take care not to waste it. It is important to have fun, but we must not neglect self improvement and planning for future. By wisely managing your options and goals, in other words by proper choice, you can achieve much more, and be much happier as a result.

Proper choice can also be important in distinction between virtue and flaw/vice. We choose every day between actions that will reinforce good or bad habits. In Plato's and Aristotle's ethics, virtue is achieved by habitual virtuous acts. If you keep doing acts of courage, you will become courageous, if you keep indulging your aggressive impulses, you will become violent. If you make it a habit to exercise you will become strong. If you study by habit you will become knowledgeable.

This can be used for the purpose of this book by making it a habit to think in terms that will make you feel more confident and in terms that reinforce the will for self improvement. Think of a way to improve your general wellbeing and health. Study new areas of expertise, develop your talents, practice new skills, plan well what you do with your money in order to gain the most benefit from it, do physical exercises, eat healthier food, etc. On the other hand it is important to avoid thinking in terms that make you feel irritated, angry, sad, or victimized by others. Such thoughts will gradually make you feel offended by the slightest discomfort caused by other people, even non intentional. In addition, avoid thinking about things that make you lose your good habits. Start by gradually changing your habits and the way of thinking. It is difficult to maintain a drastic change longterm, but changing one thing at a time is manageable. The main goal is to establish a habit and break the routine. Once you start to change it is easier keep going.

"You cannot quench understanding unless you put out the insights that compose it. But you can rekindle those at will, like glowing coals. I can control my thoughts as necessary; then how can I be troubled? What is outside my mind means nothing to it. Absorb that lesson and your feet stand firm."[24] – You will not be bothered if you remove what bothers you from your mind.

This quote fits very well with the contents of this book. As it was mentioned, the negative emotional reactions are frequently caused by people or events that displease us. If we remove the

---

24 Ibid. book 7, par. 2

irritating thought from our mind we will remove the cause of irritation. So, by controlling your thoughts you also control your emotions. If the problem at hand is not something vital for our life, there is no reason to bother with it. It can be safely discarded. This concept will be explained in the next chapter.

"It can ruin your life only if it ruins your character. Otherwise it cannot harm you—inside or out."

This quote has a similar meaning to the former: Bad influence can only harm you if you let it change your character for the worse, if it changes your mentality. Misfortune in life will only ruin you if you let it break your spirit.

"When you have to deal with someone, ask yourself: What does he mean by good and bad? If he thinks x or y about pleasure and pain (and what produces them), about fame and disgrace, about death and life, then it shouldn't shock or surprise you when he does x or y. In fact, I'll remind myself that he has no real choice."[25]

People act according to their worldview and their ethics. If you know their principles you will not be surprised by their actions. It is very similar with other things: if you know the laws that govern them you will be able to predict how will they behave. For example, if you are familiar with economics you will be able to understand the state of the market and its changes. You truly

25   Ibid. book 8, par. 14

know someone or something only if you know the rules that govern their behavior.

> *"Don't waste the rest of your time here worrying about other people—unless it affects the common good. It will keep you from doing anything useful. You'll be too preoccupied with what so-and-so is doing, and why, and what they're saying, and what they're thinking, and what they're up to, and all the other things that throw you off and keep you from focusing on your own mind. You need to avoid certain things in your train of thought: everything random, everything irrelevant. And certainly everything self-important or malicious."* [26]

– Do not collect or spread gossip. Do not do things without a purpose.

This quote fits well as an extension of the former quotes. Thinking about what others say, think, and do is a waste of time. Do not concern yourself with their private lives. It does not matter what are their religious or political beliefs, their gender, race, or sexual orientation. It does not matter what kind of assets they own and how they acquired them. It does not matter what they think of us. If their words or deeds offend us, we must remember they are irrelevant. We should spend our time and energy on self improvement and important matters in our own life. There is no use in collecting idle gossip and trivial information about other people. Do not trouble yourself with their bitter remarks and crude jokes aimed at "wrong-thinkers". Do not compare yourself

26 Ibid. book 3, par. 4

to others unless it is something positive that will make you work harder. Avoid activities imposed on you by peers and society if they have no purpose or meaning to you, i.e. irrelevant social events, ceremonies, traditional customs, marriage, relationships, buying expensive things you do not really want or need.

"Now they see you as a beast, a monkey. But in a week they'll think you're a god—if you rediscover your beliefs and honor the logos."[27] – It is never too late to change.

This quote can be interpreted in three ways: People will consider you a fool if you do not do as they do.

On the other hand, an interpretation more fitting to this book would be: People who considered you a fool for being different will change their opinion if you become successful by following your own way.

Third interpretation could be, if you change for the better, you will regain the respect of others.

People who live as everyone else does rarely achieve something noteworthy. Whatever you do, you should change for the sake of your own wellbeing, not to fit in with others.

"Ignoring what goes on in other people's souls—no one ever came to grief that way. But if you won't keep track of what your own soul's doing, how can

---

27 Ibid. book 4, par 16

you not be unhappy?"[28]

"People try to get away from it all—to the country, to the beach, to the mountains. You always wish that you could too. Which is idiotic: you can get away from it anytime you like. By going within. Nowhere you can go is more peaceful—more free of interruptions—than your own soul."[29] – Happiness is found inside you, not outside.

Here we go back to what was written at the entrance to the Oracle of Delphi: know yourself. In Stoic philosophy, to study your soul is to study reason. Philosophy itself and question of human condition come from there. Only self improvement and self knowledge bring general wellbeing and resulting happiness.

Even if you have all the best that you may wish for, all the riches in the world, or the best and the most beautiful love partner; even if you are the most powerful person in the world you will not be happy if you do not know how to appreciate it. You must know how to be satisfied with what you have, otherwise you will never have enough and your wishes will never be fulfilled. Conversely, if your life is filled with troubles, you can still be satisfied with the good things you have, if only you develop suitable mentality. Therefore, if you want to be happy, you must develop the mentality that promotes happiness. In a more Stoic sense, you will be happy if you nurture your soul (mind, reason), if you cultivate your virtue.

28 Ibid. book 2, par. 8
29 Ibid. book 4, par. 3

"[...]the longest-lived and those who will die soonest lose the same thing. The present is all that they can give up, since that is all you have, and what you do not have, you cannot lose."[30]

Stop drifting. You're not going to re-read your Brief Comments, your Deeds of the Ancient Greeks and Romans, the commonplace books you saved for your old age. Sprint for the finish. Write off your hopes, and if your well-being matters to you, be your own savior while you can.[31] – Change begins now.

If we want to achieve something significant we must start now. There is no later. If you keep delaying you will never start working. Making a better future starts in the present. Make use of your limited time in life. Do not let a single day pass without doing at least *something* useful for yourself. Figuratively speaking, you can rest a day or two, but do not let three days pass without self improvement. Read at least a paragraph in a book, do five push-ups, meditate for five minutes, study for 5 minutes, etc. This will gradually form a habit to work daily. As you increase the effort over the time you will accomplish much more. Later, when you look back you will see how much you have improved.

"Our inward power, when it obeys nature, reacts to events by accommodating itself to what it faces—to what is possible. It needs no specific material. It pursues its own aims as circumstances allow; it turns obstacles into fuel. As a fire overwhelms what would have quenched a lamp. What's

---
30 Ibid. book 2, par. 14
31 Ibid. book 3, par. 14

thrown on top of the conflagration is absorbed, consumed by it—and makes it burn still higher."[32] – Acting reasonably solves problems.

This quote as expressed here is a combination of Nietzschean and Stoic philosophy. As it was said before, to act according to nature is to act according to reason. That way you have realistic goals and expectations, so it is easier to adapt to circumstances. Nietzschean part is getting stronger by surpassing obstacles in life.

"Not what your enemy sees and hopes that you will, but what's really there."[33] – Do not let hatred and vengefullness cloud your judgment.

Always strive to think clearly. Reduce the impact of emotions on your thought process to the minimum. Only this will help you see through deception and help you solve the problem at hand. People who dislike or hate you for whatever reason and actively make your life difficult want you to agonize over their actions. They want you to waste your time and suffer while thinking about them. The best "revenge" is to be successful and to forget about them.

"Two kinds of readiness are constantly needed: (i) to do only what the logos of authority and law directs, with the good of human beings in mind; (ii) to reconsider your position, when someone can set you straight or convert you

32 Ibid. book 4, par. 1
33 Ibid. book 4, par. 11

*to
his. But your conversion should always rest on a conviction that it's right, or benefits others—nothing else. Not because it's more appealing or more popular."*[34] – Avoid debates and pointless arguments.

Concerning your general beliefs about objective reality, only facts matter. It does not matter *who* is right or wrong, only *what* is right. In a conversation think only about what you really know about a topic, and about learning more from the conversation. State the facts you know but do not insist on them and do not defend your position. It is a waste of time and energy to argue with people. Most of them do not care about the truth, but only about being right. The truth does not require defense. Facts are facts regardless of what anyone may think or believe.

Concerning the discussions in general, they should be used as a way to learn, to search for new ideas, and to challenge your own opinions. Discussion should not turn into a debate. Debates are essentially anti-philosophic because they do not serve to expose the truth but to convince the audience that you are right. It matters not who is right or wrong, only what is true. There is no need to prove anything to anyone. It is a waste of time to talk to people who do not know how to calmly discuss a topic but immediately start arguing. There is nothing to "discuss" with them except triviality.

Concerning personal lifestyle, philosophy and ethics, there are

---

34 Ibid. book 4, par. 12

no necessarily true or false judgments. There is no rational choice in every case. The choice between two preferred goods (i.e. two types of healthy food, or between studying or exercising), or two indifferents (i.e. choice of clothes or passtime) is a matter of preference rather than reason. It could be said that it is more rational to choose an alternative that is more useful at the moment, but neither of the choices is intrinsically better than the other. When choosing and activity consider advantage and disadvantage, what is useful or harmful. Shape your mentality and philosophy to promote your general wellbeing, your physical and mental health, physical and mental abilities.

There is also a great example of stoic philosophy in *The Book of Five Rings* by Musashi Miyamoto:

"The mindset in the Way of combat must be no different from one's normal state of mind. In the course of your daily life, and when engage in strategy, there should be no whatsoever in your outlook. Your mind should be expansive and direct, devoid of tension, but not at all casual. Keep your mind centered, not leaning too much to one side, swaying serenely and freely so that it does not come to a standstill in moments of change. Consider this carefully. The mind is not static even in times of calm. In times of haste the mind does not rush. The body does not carry the mind and the mind does not carry the body. The mind should be vigilant when the body is exposed. The mind must not be absent nor excessive. Both the high-spirited mind and the lethargic mind are a

sign of weakness."[35]

Even though the book speaks mainly about warfare and combat, it is useful for everyday life because the principles are valid for every form of conflict. This specific quote expresses the Stoic attitude in several sentences. It advises to maintain the stoic calm and control of your inner state in both normal and stressful situations. If you feel emotionally/mentally down, it should not affect your body. Conversely, if you feel tired or physically ill it should not affect your mind, like it is sad in the following quote. In more general terms, if you face the challenge of annoying people in your life regardless of the situation, be they your boss, a spouse, a verbal bully, random bystander, a friend, a family member, etc, you will grow stronger through conflict. If you do not strive to overcome these challenges you will grow meek and will be trodden upon by those who see you as an easy target. It does not matter if you will respond to these people in any way, the only important thing is maintaining the attitude that promotes calm. With strong mentality it is much easier to achieve your goals in life than with a mentality of a victim promoted by social justice warriors and feminists.

"Like that. In illness—or any other situation. Not to let go of philosophy, no matter what happens; not to bandy words with crackpots and philistines—

[35] Miyamoto, M. 2018, *The Book of Five Rings,* Tuttle publishing, Boston, The Water Scroll (1).

good rules for any philosopher. Concentrate on what you're doing, and what you're doing it with."[36]

After all that had been said, this one does not need any further explanations.

Rationalization

Negative reactions are frequently caused by provocations, different opinions and ideologies, rudeness of coworkers and friends, human stupidity, etc. To increase mental discipline we must learn to control our emotional reactions. In addition to subconscious processes, emotions also stem from conscious thought process. The most important factor in the thought process is general knowledge and understanding. This relates back to what was said about wisdom. Understanding of the world and people who live in it comes from theoretical knowledge, philosophic reflection, and formal education combined with personal experience. Lack of general knowledge is a form of modern decadence. Despite all the benefits of the Internet, easily accessible books, and information in general people still do not know enough and do not study enough. Wisdom and knowledge is important because they support the process of rationalization.

---

36 Aurelius, M., 2003, *Meditations*, Modern Library, New York, book 9, par. 41

They provide understanding that is used to change your perspective by rationalizing matters that cause your emotional distress.

Formal and informal education actualize the inborn potential of an individual. Unfortunately, formal education, especially state funded education does not always promote critical thinking. You cannot make a fully developed adult person to think what you want by force, but you can use mass media to gradually shape their worldview. Education can be used to indoctrinate people from young age. It is difficult to remove effects of indoctrination. Indoctrinated individuals will not question their beliefs even when faced with firm evidence to the contrary. We can all witness this when either talking to such persons or by watching recorded interviews with such individuals. Public, state funded education aims to produce an obedient worker, a soldier, a tax-paying voting drone instead of a free thinking person. In some countries religious institutions are mixed up in the system of education which escalates the problem even further. This is why we must rely on informal education, we must study on our own to actualize our potential and to undo the harm of formal education, if it exists. No one can cover all the possible fields of knowledge, but we can all strive towards original thought. We should not just accept the way of life of average people as the ideal, because customs and tradition they follow get outdated before you know it. We must strive not to take for granted what we are taught by authority figures like parents, teachers, politicians, priests, and media. We must think about it critically to determine to what degree are they saying the truth and to what degree is it useful for us and the society in general.

If a naturally intelligent person receives no education or poor education, that person will be average at best and stupid at worst. On the other hand, if a naturally not very bright person receives proper education, their natural handicap will at least be reduced so that they can function in a society among the average people. Another benefit of education is in the fact that it promotes abstract thinking, which goes double for philosophy. Without abstract thinking a person is unable to draw the essence from studied material or conversations. They are unable to understand ideas, concepts, and patterns of behavior.

For example, politician and theologians alike tend to deliberately avoid expressing the point clearly and precisely. They want to mislead and to confuse by going in circles instead of answering the question. They avoid key terms and talk down to people by using oversimplified language like they are talking to children. You will notice this if you have enough general knowledge and if you listen attentively.

Another example are the people who read mechanically. If you ask them what did they learn from a read material, they will tell you bits of superficial data, but they will be unable to briefly sum it up to express the point. When reading it is important to read attentively and to reflect on what was read to connect all the elements. If you just mechanically read the words or sentences, you will miss the general idea.

The role of philosophy in education is to provide a method of study and thought which helps to understand the point of particular material, to abstract its essence, as well as see how it fits in the subject of study as a whole and in the everyday life in its practical application.

People who lack wisdom, in other words knowledge and understanding will react very negatively when faced with people and events they cannot, and do not want to understand. This is primarily the case with extreme ideological differences, like being an atheist in front of a person profoundly influenced by religion, while milder differences may provoke only laughter or antipathy. It is a natural instinct to form prejudice based on your worldview, to judge depending on what is familiar to you. Some people react with strong surprise, anger, fear, or hatred when faced with what they consider unacceptable. They are unable to comprehend how can someone think and behave differently than they do. They may even feel threatened. They formed their worldview among people who think the same as they do and they never stopped to think about other perspectives. They do not even think deeply about their own perspective, let alone trying to understand others. It is simple to draw analogy and conclude that just like they have their own interests and opinions, so do other people. They do not have to agree with each other but they should at least be able to accept the difference as the real state of things. As long as it does no harm to anyone it should not really matter.

The mental state of anger, hate, and confusion described here may seem absurd to some readers, but there are many people who behave that way so it is important to mention it if for no other reason, then to explain the stoic concept of wisdom. It is an important part of mental discipline to develop self control and conquer the described weakness of strong emotional reactions to words and actions of others. Another frequent causes of strong emotions are vanity, arrogance, cowardice, greed, lust, and similar flaws. Some people will abandon all reason in blind pursuit of their desires. This is a similar state to strong reaction to opposing opinion or to provocation. In both cases a person is unable to control their emotions and urges.

The more wise you are, in stoic/philosophic sense, the better you will understand the motivation behind actions and thoughts of other people. This will help you remain calm and indifferent towards different opinions and ideologies because you know and understand what they stand for and how they came to be. If you disagree with them it makes no difference to you since it does not come as a surprise. And more importantly, it neither influences your life, nor it threatens you. In other words, you must learn about different philosophies, religions, politics, etc. in order to understand why people think and behave the way they do, as mentioned before. In that case you will not feel strongly about the differences. Wisdom and knowledge on worldly matters does not bring only calm and indifference in interpersonal relations, it is also of inestimable use to ensure your material wellbeing through rational management of your assets, and spiritual wellbeing by appreciation of art, philosophy, literature, and new ideas.

These benefits are the reason why development of wisdom through study is the best way to start developing the stoic calm. Another, faster but less rewarding way is to develop a disinterest in people as a habit. It takes a lot of time and energy to study, but it takes much less to develop a disinterest. This might be the best course for those who do not have enough time for thorough study of mentioned subjects. Disinterest eliminates a significant part of stress caused by peer pressure and irrelevant personal information that people tend to share. Stress of peer pressure is caused if a person cares a lot about opinion of their peers and colleagues at school or at workplace. If you are disinterested in these people, their opinion will have less impact on you whether it is positive or negative. Another cause of peer pressure is self-image. People want to be appreciated by others. This need and peer pressure it causes is solved by internal validation which will be explained later.

In the case of insults and provocations, you should keep in mind that they serve only to throw you out of balance. They serve to make you open to some form of emotional attack. If you respond to them you lose. Some people, especially men, will do all sorts of self-destructive actions when provoked, like Marty from *Back to the Future* when called chicken. In these cases people who provoke you just want to have fun by demeaning you. The same can be said about rudeness and insults. People use them in order to vent out their frustrations on others. They try to demean other people in order to feel better about themselves. As mentioned before, when faced with different way of life, people feel their own way is threatened so they try to transfer the pressure they feel onto others to make them conform. In other cases people will aim at your pride to pressure you into doing something either harmful for you or beneficial to them, like a favor. For example if a woman wants something from a man, she will "educate" him on what a "real man" is and what he should do. That way she will aim at his pride to shame him into doing her a favor. This concept can be used in wide variety of ways. You just need to find a personal weakness and aim at it. Tactics like these are often used by politicians and media, especially those labeled as conservative. When they want to make men silent and more obedient, they tell them to man up and take risks of having family, to work difficult and/or dangerous jobs, to pay taxes, to join the army, to do whatever else may be of use to their political agenda. This is why we must take care to understand what our weaknesses are so that we can conquer them and avoid being used as a tool.

It takes a significant amount of understanding and restraint to be truly indifferent to an "itchy" subject. Depending on your personality and preference you can become indifferent to many different things, but these three (provocations, different ideologies, and human stupidity) seem to be the most important as people tend to be the most sensitive to them. Emotional reactions in these cases are more of an instinct. As an abstract concept indifference is difficult to describe but it will be clear once you reach that state through training. Simply put, it means not to care, to be emotionally unmoved by a topic or an event. To observe things in emotionally neutral terms.

In terms of Stoicism, rationalization of a situation and basic understanding of people give you helpful theoretical knowledge, but it takes experience to be sufficiently wise to be indifferent.

This experience is gained through application of Stoicism in everyday life and through mental training which causes emotions and thoughts to run significantly less wild in comparison to an untrained person. It is necessary to develop an attitude of indifference through training and experience so that you do not get irritated by instinct. This attitude is useful in resisting the annoyance of everyday grind caused by people in your surroundings, be they family, friends, or colleagues. It is especially useful when you need to make quick and important decisions so it is necessary to remain calm and rational. Rationalization may seem like empty words, and it is, if applied unskillfully, but the skill which makes it generally useful for everyone, namely autosuggestion, will be explained later in this chapter.

Another mentioned stoic goal is to change and stabilize the inner state. The inner state that should be changed is the emotional state, and that state which people want to change is negative, unpleasant state. This relates back to what was said before about irritating subjects of different ideologies and provocations. By using that example the concept of stoic wisdom is partially explained. In essence, by accumulating knowledge and experience we become less prone to prejudice and bias which cause strong emotional reactions like confusion, anger, fear, envy, hate, etc. By practicing restraint we become immune, or at least resistant to instinctual irritation caused by things we dislike and people that want to annoy us.

A way to practice restraint is to learn how to relax mentally. Do not try to resist irritation by force. Do not focus on it and think strongly about what irritates you. Instead try to accept it and let it flow. Just observe what you feel by introspection. This will cause the change from active thinking mental state to a more relaxed and passive, introspective-meditative state. This state allows you to analyze what bothers you and to change your thought pattern so that you are not irritated by instinct as mentioned before. It is similar with physical discomfort. If you are hungry, cold, hot, or in pain, do not try to fight it with your mind. You will only feel the discomfort more intensely. Instead let it flow inside you. That way it will not feel as intense. This is a simple method to practice restraint and to control your thoughts. The concept will become more clear in the second chapter that deals with meditation.

The next important part of stoic inspired concept of living according to reason is internal validation. A frequent cause of negative or positive emotional state is the opinion of one's peers and authority figures, regardless of who they may be. An average person will feel positive emotions if complimented or praised by family members, friends, teachers, colleagues, or complete strangers. If the average person is scolded in some way, or even overhears a bad comment that they identify with, they will feel negative emotions. To become completely indifferent, or at least partially indifferent to opinions of others, one must learn how to change their inner state. The first method for that, as mentioned before, is developing knowledge and wisdom through study and rational thinking, or developing disinterest towards others. Second part of changing the inner state is rationalization closely related to the first part. Inner validation depends on your values and principles. If being appreciated and accepted by others is the most important to you, you neglect your own life and happiness in attempt to please everyone else. If you sacrifice your self-respect and self-interest in the process of pleasing others, you will only achieve the opposite of what you hoped for. It is more useful to focus on your own life and wellbeing first while taking care of social bonds with deserving people. Those who just want to take advantage of you are better forgotten.

The attitude towards opinions of others should be governed by truth. To move towards internal validation, similarly to rationalization, you do not focus on emotional aspect of opinions but rational aspect. Concerning the mental attitude alone, it does not matter what are the contents of their statement, but if the contents are true or false. Mental attitude in this case is the way you deal with outside influences, the way you choose to perceive them. If someone directs a negative but true critique towards you, it is rational to use the info for self improvement. It is irrational just to get offended without thinking. By focusing on the truth of an opinion directed towards you, you ensure higher stability of your inner state. When faced with hostility, again truth does not matter much. For example, if someone deliberately insults you, you can choose to feel offended or victimized. On the other hand you can ignore this instinct and choose to look for a reason behind the insult to determine your next action. You can even laugh it off in their face in the process. Maybe you did something wrong, maybe they have a poor sense of humor, maybe they just do not like you, or they vent their frustrations at a first available target.

In the first case you let yourself be swayed by the flow of the situation, you passively react to the stimuli. In the former case you take the initiative, you choose the way you react to the stimuli. Similar to the example of provocations, you pause for a second to create an opening for thinking instead of emotional reaction by reflex. On the outside it may seem that it is the Stoic way to passively go with the flow, but on the inside one must be able to choose their emotional reaction in order to maintain the inner peace and stability. If other people's words and actions offend you, it does not matter even if they are in the wrong. You alone are responsible for your thoughts, actions, and your inner state. For the sake of your wellbeing and mental health, it is imperative to learn how to be indifferent and to control your emotions effectively.

If you can be indifferent when facing an irritating, obnoxious fool, that alone is important, that is the essence of mental discipline and stoic indifference. What will you do next is irrelevant for this topic. The stoic way is to be determined in your intention and belief when you are certain that you are right despite the outside influences, while the way of weak individuals is to passively go with the flow and be, in this case, offended or victimized.

Developing a stoic mentality plays an important role in avoiding the problems of searching for unnecessary attention. A vital aspect of stoic mentality, and also the philosophic thinking in general, is internal validation. The need for attention and the approval of others is caused by external validation. This means that an individual bases his self-worth on outside influences, specifically on how others perceive him. Everyone has an inborn need to be accepted and valued by others. This is a natural instinct since humans are social animals.

It starts from childhood with the need of children to please their parents in order to be validated by them. Later it develops through the need to be accepted by peers and teachers as a natural part of growing up in society. If a person does not develop their psychology and affirms their self worth, their need to be accepted will have too much influence on their behavior. They will sacrifice their self-respect and self-interest in hope of acceptance. Thus a person remains naive and vulnerable to manipulation in adult age. Instead of being independent and having their own agency, they constantly seek approval and guidance from others.

The stoic way is to be indifferent, to maintain a neutral mental stance towards how other people perceive us. This does not mean to stubbornly ignore whatever others say to you, but to be as realistic as possible in estimation of facts. It means to think for yourself what is, or is not good for you and to take responsibility if you make a mistake. It does not matter if you are as good or as bad as other people say. The fact is that you have a specific quality. In order to estimate that quality accurately you must maintain an emotionless observation. In other words, you must maintain stoic indifference.

The problem of the individual with external validation of self worth is in the fact that he is willing to do almost anything for scraps of positive attention, which puts him at the mercy of other people. Internal validation, on the other hand, puts the self worth into the hands of the individual himself. Self worth, in that case, is based on personal abilities, goals, self improvement, and his rational estimation. The estimation of self worth can certainly be exaggerated and flawed, but that can be fixed with self improvement. Only a person with internal validation can have a real self respect, and only the one who respects himself will be respected by others.

Another useful principle in evaluation of judgment of other people, along with truth, is their intention. Understanding their motivation will explain their actions. Motivation is important to know because people are more prone to emotional reactions when faced with the unknown, i.e. radically different people. Understanding people in this case is also the aspect of wisdom in indifference. Even though they may not be annoying out of malevolence but personal weakness, they are still bothering you. If the person is trying to manipulate you or simply demean you in order to feel better about themselves, it does not matter if what they are saying is true or not. In that case you should be on guard and not allow them to verbally abuse you. Do not let yourself be provoked, or feel offended or angry. Think about their motivation instead of thinking how they make you feel annoyed or angry. Strive to keep calm by thinking in emotionally neutral terms. In everyday life, away from home or workplace, such provocateurs can be simply laughed off because they cannot grind on your nerves day after day as your coworkers and family members can do. In the case of people you are forced to be around, if you want to react, you should do it with a cool head and "strike" where it hurts the most. Depending on the case, a few well chosen, well deserved words will get them off your back. If verbal conflict of any kind will get you in trouble with the law or your superiors, which gets more frequent in some countries because of modern politics, it the best to ignore them with the help discipline until you can change the workplace or habitat.

These simple examples are not good enough to cover the full complexity of possible life situations, but they serve the purpose of depicting the basic concept of looking for the truth within a given situation instead of taking its general appearance as real state of things. The main point is: if someone says something that is true, there is no reason to get upset because it is true. And if the said is false, there is no reason to get upset because it is not true. If you make a mistake, getting angry, sad, or frustrated will not fix it. Do not make a big deal out of it, just avoid doing it again. That is the attitude or a point of view from which the situation is looked upon objectively and indifferently in a stoic manner. Focusing on rational estimation of the circumstances and binding self-worth on your own judgment leads towards freedom from outside influences. On the opposite side, self-worth based on opinions and expectations of others leads towards mental slavery and unhappiness. It can be very hard to please even one person, let alone everyone around you. In that case the best option is to focus on your own interest and people that really matter to you, or no one else but yourself.

Concerning what others think or say about us in general, their opinion or words themselves are irrelevant with the exception of slander. If their words and opinions bring you no real harm they do not matter. There are very few important people in life, the vast majority are a nuisance and a distraction. It does not matter if they hate you or love you, and if they do not bother you it matters even less. Taking into consideration opinions of secondary people is a waste of time and energy. The only important thing is self-knowledge so that you can change for sake of self-improvement and your own wellbeing, not for sake of being generally liked or appreciated. Popularity is only a positive side effect of success, not its cause. This mentality based on internal validation reinforces the resistance to outside influences.

To look for truth in everyday situations is a useful concept to follow when shaping your mentality. You should be interested mainly in facts and useful information, while avoiding gossip and unreliable data. It is primarily intended for personal attitude and development. An exception can be made when dealing with difficult people. In that case the truth is irrelevant, because such people do not wish to listen to reason. If you decide to engage them in an argument, you need to use *eristics*, not logic or common sense. Eristics are sophist tactics intended primarily to win a debate, not to determine the truth of arguments or to reach an agreement. Such arguments can contribute very little to personal development. If you really must do it, maybe professionally, books that could be of use on the topic are, among the others, *Eristic Dialectic* by Schopenhauer, *Art of War* by Sun Tzu, and *The Book of Five Rings* by Musashi Miyamoto. There are certainly other books of use on this topic but these are the classics, with *Eristic Dialectic* being one of the best, if not *the* best.

In the most cases it is pointless or counterproductive to argue, especially if you are exposed to irrational nagging of bosses, parents, teachers, and others of whom you may depend. In these cases, if you cannot afford to distance yourself from these people, the situation becomes the battle of attrition. This is where Stoicism comes to its greatest use, and its greatest test. The aim is to become unaffected by their words. This can be very difficult to achieve, but not impossible. To reach this stage, it is necessary to gradually develop your personality towards that goal. Most of the elements that constitute personality are formed by habit. As many philosophers of ancient Greece believed, virtue is achieved by habit and training. It could be said that being virtuous is the same as being well trained, not necessarily trained physically but rather mentally.

To achieve the virtue of stoic firmness and emotional immobility, it is important to avoid thinking in the way that makes you irritated, angry, offended, or otherwise out of balance. You should strive to examine every situation, especially a stressful situation in a neutral, objective terms that describe the situation as it is instead of adding either positive or negative connotations. Less important and less stressful situations are suitable for initial training of these skills.

For example, if you happen to overhear people talking nonsense, or they are just being loud and annoying, instead of focusing on the way they are irritating you, try to block them out by thinking about something more useful. For example, you can think about what will you do when you get home, which of your duties you already solved and which ones still need to be done. Think about something you find interesting, a book, a topic, an article. Whatever it is, it is certainly better than wasting your time and energy on thinking about annoying, random bystanders. The same is valid for likes of acquaintances and colleagues you find annoying. If they do not talk to you directly why even think about them? It gives you no benefit. This is just a simple example but it is useful to illustrate the basic concept. Strive in every situation to maintain your composure so that you develop a habit and an aptitude for it. That way you will gradually become more resistant to stress of any type and you will be able to maintain your indifference and objectivity in mentally demanding situations.

Habit

Personality traits and habits are among the things that people tend to be unhappy with. Habit is formed by routine repetition of an action. It is a powerful force in human life. Figuratively speaking, mastering the habit means mastering yourself. Personality itself is just a collection of habits, a collection of nurtured tendencies formed in the process of growing up. It is true that many of our traits are inborn, but the majority are the matter of habit. Illness, problems, and lack of success in life are often a product of lifelong bad habits. Deeply rooted habits can be hard to break, but not impossible. If you deliberately continuously cancel the execution of routine actions, the habit will gradually weaken and cease to exist. How fast and easy is this to accomplish, depends on how determined and disciplined you are.

For example, obese people in the most cases, have bad habits which cause their condition, such as eating unhealthy food and lack of physical activity. These bad habits can be broken if they choose to substitute their usual food with something healthier. This may be a problem as people tend to perceive it as inconvenient. Maybe because it is out of their way, they cannot decide on what else to eat, or they are simply too lazy to think and to try to change the habit in the first place. Simply planning a change instead on dwelling on the problem may be a good step to achieve the goal. The next step is to seize the initiative when you feel like implementing the plan before you get second thoughts.

It is the same with exercising, the biggest problem is to break the habit of inaction. Starting to take short walks, or doing a few basic exercises daily such as crunches, push-ups, squats or at least simple dynamic stretching can be a good way to start a good habit. After the start it is only a matter of persistence to achieve your goal by gradually substituting bad habits for good habits.

Personality traits are very similar to habits because they can be formed by performing actions repeatedly, as it was said in the theory of Stoicism. For example, if you keep trying to understand others you will become understanding or compassionate. If you judge them without thinking about their position you will become judgmental. Personality traits also depend on fundamental values and principles that an individual had adopted. They represent your pre-formed views and they govern your behavior and thought process. As such they play an important role in habits you develop. Principles and values are formed by philosophic thinking and may vary between each individual to a high degree. They will be explained in detail later in this chapter.

Another important part of personality traits are instincts and emotions that you choose to encourage by acting upon them and by paying attention to them. If you deliberately do not act upon instincts and emotions considered undesirable, with time and perseverance their intensity will be reduced and eventually they may cease to exist. However, if you keep paying attention to these instincts and emotions, if you keep feeling their effects, if you immerse in them, but still do not act on them, they will only turn into frustration. So, do not try to change your habits by force. The key is not only avoid acting on them but to calmly accept them, or to change your inner state so they do not bother you. You can either simply think about something else, or think about why are these actions harmful and convince yourself not to do it. It can also be useful to distract yourself with a productive hobby so that bad habits do not cross your mind. This is just a starting point and the basic theory. Concrete mechanisms for changing your habits will be explained later in the book.

Personality traits such as bad temper are also formed by habit. If you keep reacting with anger to whatever displeases you to the slightest, you will keep acting that way simply because you are used to it and anger will arise automatically in such situations. To break these habits it is important to think rationally instead of reacting by instinct. If you feel angered do not act instantly but think instead if it is really something to be angered about, does it really matter, is it important, which correlates to what was said before about rationally estimating the situation to change your inner, emotional state.

In any attempt to change a habitual action, it is vital not to let the emotions sway you in the wrong direction. Once the goal is achieved, people tend to relax and stop their effort which often leads to restoration of the bad habit. For that matter it is important to persist in their new activity until it is deeply rooted in the subconsciousness, especially if the bad habit had been severe. Only then it will become effortless to live in the new way and the risk of relapse will be insignificant.

Concerning the change of inner state, it is also possible to change it in order to conform with the society. Which means to change the way of thinking and the behavior in accordance with social norms, to avoid standing out, or any discomfort or conflict with people. That way of adapting to one's surroundings is certainly easier but it is ill advised. Conformism does not lead to mental discipline and freedom but to mental slavery. The aim is not to conform, but to resist influences that cause conformism, or simply put, to be indifferent to outside influences.

There is nothing that cannot be changed in one's personality. Every part of it is only a matter of habit, choice, or principle. All these things can be changed if one is willing. Gradual change starting from weak habits towards stronger ones is much more effective than sudden changes of core habits. So, change a bad habit for a useful one. Start small by swapping elements of your routine: change one unhealthy snack or food type in your meals for a healthier alternative, drink tea instead of coffee, slowly reduce the amount of salt or sugar you add in food, stop putting sugar in coffee or tea altogether, drop a byword and adopt a new random one, etc. Make one change at a time and wait for a while until it settles before introducing a new one. Many examples of gradual changes in thought patterns have already been mentioned in this chapter. Changes in habits that constitute your mentality have the strongest impact on developing mental discipline. After a while of deliberate transformation, when you reflect on your progress you will notice you have become a completely new person without realizing it.

Auto-suggestion

Concepts mentioned so far sound very simple, yet when it comes to practical application, they may prove to be ineffective. That brings the topic of difference between *thinking* and *auto-suggestion*. Just thinking the proposition "there is no reason for this to bother me" makes little or no impact on inner state or emotion. Willing it to be so while thinking the proposition, with a little practice, is what makes this method of controlling emotions effective.

Auto-suggestion is a command to yourself thought with conviction. To influence yourself in this way is one of the easiest and the most basic skills one should learn in order to gain mental discipline and effective control of emotions. It is a starting skill that helps to find the mental mechanism to shape your emotions by willpower, which will be explained further in following chapters. It is similar to what was said about using stoic advice to your benefit, it is important to view it as true with determination. By accepting the advice as part of your subjective reality and world-view you change your inner state. The difference here is in the fact that you are not learning from other people's advice. You do not search for the mentioned realization or objective philosophic truth, but you use your will to change your inner state by "force". Learning from Stoics is shaping your mentality according to worldview and, in gaming terms, a passive ability. Auto-suggestion is an active, flexible ability used to change your inner state whenever it is required. It does not need to rely on what you perceive as a general principle or truth, but what you need at the moment. It is used when your passive indifference cannot handle the stimuli from outside influences. If used in accordance with your general worldview it will be more effective and it will strengthen your passive indifference to a higher degree.

To develop the skill of auto-suggestion and to learn how to influence your emotions with your mind, you should attempt to use it whenever you get an opportunity. It is a mental skill so describing exactly how to use it, how to develop it, or how it feels is impossible and useless. You can see the use of physical skills, so you use rough imitation to learn them through practice. On the contrary, to learn mental skills exercises can be only be described and not shown directly, so it is up to the practitioner to rely on their own effort and intuition. If your intuition tells you to do the exercise in a different way, it may be beneficial to try it out. Mental skills are subjective. They are not something that can be pointed at by a finger, but something that needs to be experienced. The only way to learn is by experimentation and persistence until subtle difference between simple thought and auto-suggestion is noticed. Once this is achieved, the skill is very easy to apply in the future.

A few guidelines to learn auto-suggestion:
1. Whenever you happen to be in a stressful situation, try to alleviate it by thinking something appropriate for the desired change. As mentioned before, in a situation where you feel offended by something other people say, think something like "there is no reason for this to bother me; this is true/false so I must face the uncomfortable fact/need not worry about it; These people are irrelevant to me, no point worrying about them."
2. If you are in a situation that causes anxiety, think something along these lines: "This is a good opportunity to face my fears; I am well prepared for this, I can handle anything that is about to happen; If I fail now, there is always another attempt or another option."
3. Another possibility for exercising the mentioned skill is to use such phrases as mentioned before, as mantras. Which means to repeat one of them multiple times in mind. Another way is to make up a short text in verse which may represent personal principles or some sort

of words of encouragement. To be more specific, the content of a text like that should be something that will inspire desired change in the user at any given situation.

4. For everyday situations when one wishes to practice this skill, it may be useful to try to change a fun activity to something more useful. For example if you enjoy playing video games, or watching TV, you can use auto-suggestion to change that activity to reading, physical exercise, or studying. When you are having fun it may be difficult to stop doing it, which makes it a good opportunity for practice.

5. In the effort to change a bad habit (x) for a good habit (y), think something like: "I don't like x any more, y is much more appealing."

The desired change depends on what the user exactly wants. To feel calm and at peace, happy and relaxed, angry and defensive, or completely indifferent. To be interested at something, or bored and disgusted by it. Words of "inspiration" should be chosen depending on the aim. It would be useless to describe such verses as their effect may vary from person to person. It is even possible to make up something completely meaningless and associate it with a certain intention in their mind. When it is necessary to induce the desired effect it is enough to use the made up word as an auto-suggestion. Examples of such a material are often encountered in works of fiction or religious texts. Their origin is not important and they need not necessarily be used as originally intended, but they will be effective for one's personal goals if used correctly.

For example, if a person is doing physical training at one point they will start getting tired and will feel like stopping the exercise midway even though they could still practice more without a problem. If they want to complete the exercise or go all the way and use their entire stamina for the sake of greater improvement, they must combat the urge of giving up. In that case they must replace the thought of giving up with the auto-suggestion such as: "I will press on; there is no giving up; this strain is nothing to me. I will become stronger through discomfort."

In a situation in which someone feels pressured by their peers or whoever else, the person in question should think something like: "I will do what I want; they will not force me to work against myself; I know what is good for me."

To be productive and successful it is important to maintain working habits. When someone starts neglecting their obligations or general self improvement, it is important to overcome procrastination. It is not bad to have fun, but if that is all you do, you will not achieve anything significant in life. For this goal one should think of something along these lines: "There will be enough time to have fun later; This [insert important activity] is not bad at all; Studying [insert important subject] is interesting/only temporary obligation; I must do this to achieve my goals; I like doing this."

The key to success in the endeavor of changing emotional state by using these described methods is to practice while observing the emotional state. When the exercise is done correctly and the thought is thought with intention and determination, it will become an auto-suggestion and there will be a change in the inner state. Learning to recognize when the change occurs and how exactly it was done, means that the basis of the skill is learned. At that point it is only a matter of time and interest to develop it further, and explore the possibilities of the application.

To truly stay on the right path with auto-suggestions and to be self reliant as it was shown in these examples, decisions must be tempered by reason, logic, and knowledge. If one uses auto-suggestions to persist in procrastination or doing self destructive activities despite the well meaning and good advice of people in their vicinity, the practice of auto-suggestion will be counterproductive. If you cannot learn auto-suggestion through these examples despite hard work, do not despair. Self-hypnosis from the second chapter is a different, yet more profound approach to the same topic which may be easier to learn.

Reevaluation of values

There has been significant mention of values, virtues, and principles thus far. Before considering their reevaluation, it is important to define them and their importance for mental discipline. In this context they are ethical concepts because they set up end goals and means to an end in life. They determine what will be considered acceptable or unacceptable behavior. How will you treat other people, their property, non-human animals, and nature in general. What actions will improve your life or life of others, and what would make it worse.

The concept of reevaluation of values in this book is inspired by Nietzsche's philosophy. The main principle behind the concept is considering their advantage and disadvantage, the degree at which they are useful and life-furthering. On these grounds, in his *Antichrist* Nietzsche criticized Christianity and Christian ethics (or Christian morality as he puts it) as unnatural, sick, and harmful for humanity. For example, Christianity and many other religions highly value compassion and charity. Compassion itself does not help anyone, it does not solve problems, but only increases the number of people who suffer. Charity can help people in certain conditions, but unrestrained charity makes people dependent on others instead of helping them become self reliant.

Reevaluation of values certainly does not end on the level of ethics. It can be applied in every aspect of life. In other words it can be called critical thinking. Personal philosophy is not perfect. It can constantly be improved and reevaluated. Philosophies, religions, and politics made by other people are also not perfect. It is useless to take them as a package deal. They too can be reevaluated to take only the useful concepts and ideas. If you accept them under a label, you limit yourself only to a single set of ideas. However, if you are indifferent to labels and groups, if you do not require a community to guide you, you remain free from their potentially harmful influence. The aim of the concept of reevaluation is to absorb what is useful from different ideologies while avoiding their shortcomings.

These three ethical concepts, namely virtue, principle, and value are important for developing personal ethics and philosophy which in turn define your mentality. Defining these concepts for yourself is also important for self-knowledge and evaluation of your quality and quality of others, which means they are an integral part of internal validation. They will be defined here briefly and treated later in more detail.

Ethical values can be defined as non-physical, intrinsically desirable things. They are a matter of attitude and appreciation. Values are things that a subject considers praiseworthy. They are outside the subject, or a highly appreciated attribute he possesses: freedom, knowledge, life, health, death, truth, honor, social status, power, fame, wealth, friendship, family, community.

Virtue is an intrinsically good personal attribute or a trait that a subject possesses. They are integral part of his personality/intellect or body. As such they are a matter of ability and quality: strength, knowledge, courage, perseverance, temperance, modesty, wisdom, intelligence, chastity, fear of god, faith, loyalty, curiosity, diligence. Virtue was previously defined as anything that contributes to the perfection of a being. In Aristotle's ethics it is defined as a middle point between two extremes. For example, bravery is the middle point between recklessness and cowardice.

Principle can be defined as a rule of personal conduct, or a core belief. Like values, it is a preformed decision or an attitude. In terms of metaphysics, principle is the cause of being. This loosely coincides with the former because rules can be considered the cause of conduct. Without the rule/principle one would not behave the way they do. Though many principles can be arbitrary and useful only to some people, valid ethical principles must be universal. Principles are formed based on your values and virtues. For example, if you value truth, you will strive to always be honest and tell the truth, even when its uncomfortable. You will like it when people do the same, even when they say something negative but true about you. If you value knowledge, you will always seek an opportunity to learn more by principle.

In more general terms, if you want to learn something you aim to learn its principles, like it was said before. Once you learn the principles of say, economics, you will be knowledgeable in that field. You will be able to predict changes in the market, and understand changes that may confuse others who did not study economics. So, to apply philosophy for learning in general, you actively try to figure out the principles and the essence of the object of study. If you just memorize the material, you do not necessarily understand it. Without understanding you cannot apply knowledge, so you can hardly benefit from it.

In various public debates and discussions you may hear that a non-religious person cannot have moral values or principles. It means they take religious and theistic belief as a necessary prerequisite for being moral. This is obviously false because, as ancient philosophers demonstrate once again, and even the great

Aquinas himself, it is possible to reach universal ethical values and principles by use of human reason alone[37].

Reason was also mentioned before in the Stoic theory. It is a vital concept for both ethics and personal philosophy in general. It is also one of the fundamental principles of this book, along with indifference. To understand the concept of reason as seen here, it is important to consider it "in light" of reduced intensity of emotions. This topic will be treated in detail in the following chapters. Average people let their emotions and thoughts run wild. It is natural for them to rely on them when making decisions. But this is not an option for a disciplined individual who should rely primarily on reason.

When you reach the state of reduced emotion, reduced to any intensity, you will notice a significant difference in your thought process. You will notice that some of your past actions were unproductive and unnecessary. This is primarily the case with interpersonal relations when you do something when angered, or demeaned by others. As it was mentioned before, a trained individual will stop to think first, then act afterwards. The aim is to act like that most of the time, if not always.

We should not forget the positive aspect of passion. The most positive manifestation of human emotion is creative inspiration.

---

37 Rothbard, M., 1998, *The Ethics of Liberty,* New York University Press, New York, p. 6

However, inspiration alone does not polish your work into its complete final form. Persistence, hard work, and determination is what makes the difference between an impulsive experiment and the work of art. An aspect of mental discipline is to use your positive passion and lead it towards its end with the the help of reason.

Tempering your beliefs, values, and principles by reason, and keeping in mind the purpose of your actions is very important for mental discipline. It can be said that acting reasonably is acting on purpose, while acting on impulse is irrational because it does not take purpose or necessity into consideration. You act on impulse first, then think of the consequences later. Most people act within borders of reason, or common sense. Even though they often act emotionally and irrationally, they are still humans and posses reason by nature.

In terms of ethics, when reason is not taken in consideration you get a variation of black and white morality often shown in video games or movies. You get ethics that lack depth, intensity, and furthermore common sense. It may be useful to make it simpler for the mass audience, but it is neither realistic nor satisfying for a thinking individual.

For example to get points for good in games you have to go out of your way to help people and solve both their serious and,

105

more often trivial problems. Earning the points for good is usually not done as poorly as the earning of points for evil. You have to actively go out of your way to make everyone's life miserable. You resort to everything from petty theft to genocide. You talk to everyone like an angry teenager and threaten them for trivial things. You kill people for pocket change, or for talking back to you regardless of consequences. You think in absolutes, its either your way or things get messy. Is this what evil really looks like? Of course not, this is irrational and impulsive behavior of a common, low-intelligence thug. True evil, like true good requires ideology and calm, cold, reasonable planning. It requires premeditated intention and the will to follow it through.

Theologians, with few exceptions, seem to completely disregard the existence of reason, even though it is the fundamental principle that gave humans ethics in the first place. They seem to think people would suddenly start behaving like in the gaming example. So, people who advocate theistic ethics may argue that without belief in god and its commandments, there is nothing that prevents people from crime like theft, violence, murder, rape and similar. But is this really true? If it was, human race would go extinct long before monotheism, or even before any form of religion got the chance to form. It is true that human history is violent, but without cooperation and coexistence there would be no history. Not even non-human animals are that "irrational" to kill their own species without a valid reason, with exceptions of some species. Unrestrained, murderous violence is simply unnatural to both humans and other species.

Without religious law people would certainly enjoy to a greater extent things that religion usually prohibits, like alcohol, promiscuity, prostitution, porn, drugs etc. But people still use these things on large scale, despite the influence of religion, law, and tradition. There is no reason indulging in them should be considered a crime if it is done by consenting adult individuals because there is no victim. They are considered crimes only because certain people arbitrarily decided it is so. The regulation by law is primarily a matter of politics and religion. The only real crime is the action where a victim really exists. Criminals are people who by definition do not respect the law, and no law will prevent them from doing what they want.

The vast majority of people are not criminals. Resorting to crime does not even cross their mind. They just want to live their life in peace, enjoying the fruit of their labor. Crime is dangerous and very risky. Why would you risk your life stealing and robbing people when you can work and trade with others for mutual benefit. The gain does not justify the risk. It defies common sense to go out of your way to harm others. Even if you could profit on others expense unpunished, it is much more useful to produce your own value and rely on your own abilities. After all, if everyone would prey on others there would be no one left to produce goods. Cooperation is the best way to rise the living standard and develop the best of what human race has achieved thus far in terms of economics and technology. The only form of healthy, constructive conflict is the competition on the free market of goods, services, and ideas.

An important part of mental discipline and rational thinking is developing your own set of values and principles. Before you start examining the values of society, you start with yourself. For this purpose it is necessary to be familiar at least with basics of philosophy, if not in depth knowledge. It is not as important to know its history and works of various philosophers as it is important to know how to think in a philosophical way. The difference between a philosopher and a person who only studies philosophy is in the fact that philosopher can use philosophy to improve his life, contrary to a mere student of philosophy who can only regurgitate philosophic theory. In other words, one must live philosophy, not just accumulate philosophic theory without practicing it. Philosophic thinking was partially explained at the beginning of this chapter and in the theory and application of Stoicism. It will be explained further in this part of the book.

Average people connect philosophic thinking with cryptic

speaking, unnecessary mysticism, and trying to appear "deep". That is a stereotype spread by pop culture. In some parts of the world, for example in the Balkans, philosophy is equated either with talking nonsense or with sophistry. Only philosophers appreciate the value of philosophy in that area. Philosophic way of thinking in its essence is about trying to see things for what they really are, instead of clouding them with emotions, prejudice, misconceptions, and taboos made by social conventions. It is about critical thinking instead of taking things at face value. It is about trying to understand and accurately define concepts specific to humans, like it was mentioned before: What is friendship? What is romantic relationship? What is family? What is wealth? What is good and evil? What is the purpose of your actions? – these and many similar questions can be answered with the help of philosophy. Dictionary definitions of these terms or concepts can be easily found. But what do they mean for you specifically? Are the dictionary definitions good enough? It may not be the question of objective truth but rather a matter of personal preference and attitude. It is the task of philosophy to determine if it is so.

From ancient time one of the main goals of philosophy was to seek the truth about the world, its phenomena, the nature of things, human nature, nature in general, society, people, one's self, and everything else that may be of interest. To apply this pursuit to personal life it is important to think about your experience of everyday situations. Not to dwell on them uselessly, but in order to learn something from them. Reflect on what were your actions, words, and thoughts in these situations and what was their cause. How did you respond to personal questions you were asked and why. Think hard and honestly about these questions. Do not let yourself be satisfied with superficial answers. That will help you learn more about yourself and your motivation. For example, if you happened to be rude to someone, was it because you were angry at that person, or something unrelated made you angry? If someone said something ordinary, but it made you upset. Why did it feel like that? If you were on a job interview, and you were asked the cliché question: where do you see yourself in ten years? What would you say? Do you have a clear image of what you want to achieve, an image of success, or even a plan to realize it? Even if you see yourself on a sofa watching TV, what does it represent to you? Leisure? Freedom? Pleasure?

After getting through a stressful situation, it naturally keeps returning to your mind for a while. Think about it as objectively as possible. Find the reason for your actions and thoughts. Can you remain calm and think, or do you just go with flow in such a situation? In the first case think about what helped you and how can you improve yourself to do even better next time. In the second case, think about what made it so stressful that you could not even think. Find a way to conquer your weakness through stoic philosophy and mental discipline.

Through philosophic thinking and observing your own behavior you start to develop your own ethics. You determine and define things that motivate you, your virtues and flaws. In the process of introspection you will discover some personal traits you dislike. It is important to face the truth and to change for the better, if you truly dislike those traits. Convincing yourself that you are not really like that or justifying yourself leads only to self-deception. It is more rational and much more useful to accept, or at least to acknowledge a bad personality trait without changing it than to deny its existence. That way you will at least know who or what you are. If you admit that a problem exists, you will be able to start working on solving it. This related back to famous saying attributed to Socrates: "I know that I know nothing." You are truly ready to learn only when you acknowledge your lack of knowledge. If you think you know everything in an area of expertise, what else is there to learn? It is the same with bad traits and habits. What is there to improve if you think everything is already optimal?

If you look honestly deep inside yourself, you will know that you alone are to blame for your failings. However, this does not mean you should dwell on this and be depressed. You should accept it and do better next time. It is the same if your plans really were obstructed by an outside force. If you cannot remain calm, use all your anger and frustration as energy for your motivation. Your effort does not have to be perfect, but doing something is better than helplessly steaming in your misfortune.

It is also useful to reflect on hypothetical situations you may see in a movie, read about in a book, on the Internet, in the newspaper, or situations you simply imagined. As an outside observer your view will be more objective. By thinking like that you will be able to abstract general principles and values from particular events. If you see a certain pattern of behavior you dislike, you can decide not to act that way in the future. You can get new ideas and see things from a different perspective. It is possible to encounter some of the previously mentioned existential questions. You may not like the solution proposed by the author and think of a better one, or maybe see a flaw in your own reasoning.

Thinking about such situations helps to form opinions or impressions about things in general that may be important to your life. These opinions may be wrong but they can be verified and improved later when your values and principles are tested by experience. That way you reach new conclusions based on what was learned, and it often becomes necessary to rethink your position. This is not an endless, futile process but a necessary way of personal growth. It is the way you start forming your values and principles on your own. Through your experiences you find out what works the best for you. What kind of qualities are the most effective in reaching your goals. With these goals in mind you start appreciating specific abstract concepts, behavior patterns, and thought patterns called values. You form good habits and discover positive personal traits called virtues. You also find rules that prescribe certain behaviors and prohibit other behaviors, and these rules are called principles.

Philosophic thinking is best done in solitude, especially in combination with reading something mentally stimulating. In this era of smart-phones, easily accessible Internet connection, and social networks, average people spend very little time alone. Even insignificant, short-term solitude is unbearable to the most of them. They get bored very quickly, even in company of their friends. They constantly have to check their phones for calls, e-mails, messages, memes, and comments on social networks. When they are somewhere physically alone, their mind is still in some form of social interaction. This leaves little or no time for the so called "philosophic idleness".

This idleness is not the type when you just sit down and do nothing in particular, but when you are free from other important work and you have enough time for thinking. The term originates from ancient Greece. It was one of the ideals of philosophers of that time. They considered it to be vital to ensure your material wellbeing so that you can occupy yourself with philosophy later in life. Thanks to the modern technology people have much more free time than they used to in the past, so it is possible to start with philosophic pursuits much earlier. But the ideal of idleness is still valid. In modern times it can be called a retirement plan. You aim to achieve it as soon as possible so that you can be free to do what you like and enjoy the fruits of your labor.

Solitude is very important for self-development. It eliminates distractions and allows you to focus on your thoughts. This focus causes deeper, more introspective and meditative thinking which helps you gain self-knowledge. Solitude intensifies your thought process. Your ideas becomes more original and independent. Through solitary thinking you can become more comfortable with yourself and being alone. To be comfortable alone is another factor in reducing outside influences, because you depend less on others for company. Thus you are less likely to spend time with people you dislike or to conform in order to alleviate your loneliness. Another important factor of solitude is thinking about existential questions. They arise naturally when one spends a lot of time alone. Sometimes you can hear the elderly say that while alone, "all kinds of things cross your mind". They probably start to question their lifelong beliefs. Previous generations often lived in large families with four or more children, especially in rural areas. Their lives were too full of hard work and social interactions to allow them time for thinking. But at older age they can no longer spend as much time with their friends and family, so they are faced with themselves and their own mind for the first time and it terrifies them. Philosophy is better equipped than any other science to deal with existential questions. Questions like those already mentioned, the question of purpose of life, ethical questions like do you or did you live your life properly, what does it mean to live properly in the first place? Why do you live, why do you get up in the morning? What do you think of death, do you believe in life after death or not? Does it matter to you if you will live on or cease to exist? Do you believe in existence of one or more deities? If so, how do you describe their existence, what is their nature in metaphysical terms? Are they a personal deity (do they have personality) or are they more like a cosmic force, or Nature itself? Does this fit with the religion you practice, if you do practice a religion? Do you regret doing something, or not doing it? All these and much more are existential question that you must come to terms with as soon as possible in your life, or they will come to haunt you at your old age. If you can at least take them calmly even if you do not have the answer you will be able to cope with long term solitude.

If it is too hard to be alone by choice, leave your communication devices at home and go for a walk in a park, go jogging, go for a cup of coffee, or to a library, wherever you will be able to spend time thinking. Walking is very effective in stimulating your mind. Some of the most influential philosophers liked it. For example, Aristotle's school was called Peripatetic, from Greek *peripatetikoi*, those who walk. He was going for a walk with his students while discussing philosophy. Nietzsche took regular walks in the mountains. Kant went for walks every day at the same time, even in bad weather.

It is also advisable to always have a book at hand to read while waiting for the beginning of a class, a meeting, for public transport, etc. When making appointments in your free time, leave some time for yourself. Doing a hobby alone can also be considered a form of constructive solitude, but just sitting and thinking, or reading combined with meditation is more intense.

Despite the benefits of solitude, do not forget that one man cannot do everything on his own. Learning from others through books is very useful, but discussing your ideas with other free thinking individuals will help you make the most of what you learn through books. It will help you check your ideas and understand better what you read.

To decide on what kind of virtues, values, and principles to form, it is necessary to define your end goals first. Setting up one supreme, hard, or even impossible goal to achieve for an activity, a hobby, or life in general, will do much more good for self motivation than any number of easy to achieve minor goals. Once you achieve a minor goal, the momentum that drives towards further accomplishment disappears. You need time to think of something else you want to achieve. However, if such minor goals are perceived as steps towards the supreme goal, the momentum will not be broken. You may rest for a while between the steps, but the ideal is not yet achieved. There is no need to think much what to do next. You just continue working towards it. The archetype of Stoic Sage is an example of supreme goal. The aimed goal of this book is mental discipline. As it is based on stoic philosophy it can be considered an aspect of Stoic Sage.

A common example of a minor goal, which a lot of men have, is to get fit to attract women. If they succeed or fail in that intent they stop exercising so they fall out of shape again. But if they would practice to maintain their health and physical abilities they would continue training as soon as they would start weakening.

Training or exercising for long term benefits is an example of a higher goal which can never truly be completed because you have to work on it your entire life to keep the benefits.

Another example of a minor goal is gaining the black belt in a martial art. A lot of people give up practice thinking they learned everything, but black belt only means they have grasped well the basics of the martial art. That is only the beginning towards the mastery of the art, which is an example of a higher or even supreme goal as one can spend their whole life in rigorous training.

Another minor goal in life may be earning a lot of money, or getting rich. By the time that is done, especially if it is hard earned, one may forget what were they to do with it in the first place and end up squandering it on things of little benefit. If they spend their life working for money and ruin their health, they may be too old and sick to enjoy it. Money is nothing more than a tool, or a means to achieve other things. Some people also gather a large wealth and live their whole life as if they were poor, like characters in some classic works, i.e. Aulularia by Plautus. This is the same as not having any money, because "true power lies not in wealth but in things it affords you"[38].

Setting up higher or even supreme goals in life or activities

---

38 Vampire: The Masquerade - Bloodlines, Activision, Troika, 2004. video game

that one does is what makes difference between mediocrity and significant achievement. People who keep setting up low goals will hardly realize their full potential because of halted momentum in the progress, or simple lack of ambition. One supreme goal that could cover all other goals is self improvement towards perfection in every possible area, or at least in fields of highest interest. It is a never ending quest that keeps calling with multitude of its rewards. Such a form of self improvement may not always be of material value, but the benefit of freedom and personal development is inestimable. If you have to choose between multiple options, you will do well to choose the option which leads closer to the supreme goal. Sacrificing an immediate pleasure for greater gain later is the essence of asceticism. Asceticism for the sake of itself or self-punishment without any higher purpose, however, is of no use, while asceticism for self-improvement and self-surpassing is an excellent tool.

Values were previously defined as intrinsically good non-physical things. Now it is important to name at least few values important for mental discipline. They are firstly indifference, reason, knowledge, and wisdom. These four are closely connected as strengthening one also improves the other. They have already been explained before, especially knowledge and wisdom. Indifference is a difficult concept to describe, but it is explained through numerous examples in this chapter. If one and the most important value must be named, it is indifference. Simply put, you are disciplined and indifferent when you can remain undisturbed by negative influences from your surroundings. When you think calmly and rationally without caring for negative conditions around you.

Other values of ancient philosophers and their society can also be considered useful for mental discipline. For example, temperance, diligence, rationality, objectivity, just to name a few. All these concepts can be valued by a person who relies more on reason than on emotions, they all lead to your wellbeing. However, these are just examples that put the intended goal into perspective. Readers are free to choose their own values.

How does a person make their own values? In addition to philosophic thinking mentioned before, we can learn a useful criteria for reevaluating values from Nietzsche. Similar to what he said about an opinion[39] can be said about a value: the only important question is how far a value is life-furthering and life-preserving. It does not have to be a matter of objective truth, but rather a matter of preference or usefulness. This can be a very useful criteria for forming personal values. You choose what to

---

39 Nietzsche, F., 2013, *Al di là del bene e del male,* Adelphi, Milano, chap. 1, par. 4

value and appreciate depending on your end goal. For example, if you want to achieve the before mentioned idleness, your aim is to retire early. In that case your values should be based on what helps you earn a lot of money, primarily knowledge. First and foremost knowledge of economics and philosophy, secondly any profitable skill set like programming, engineering, graphical design, mastery of any form of art or craft. Mental discipline also plays an important role in business, because an individual with focused and rational thoughts makes better decisions. With creativity and hard work you can find a way to capitalize on your abilities, earn significant amount of money, invest it wisely and retire when you have enough assets to support your lifestyle for the rest of your life. How long will this take depends on your lifestyle and your ability to earn money. In conclusion, for this kind of goal your values can be: knowledge, wisdom, discipline, creativity, diligence, temperance, wealth, freedom, tolerance, cold reason, etc.

If your goal is say, spiritual development, your values could be something else: asceticism, compassion, charity, knowledge, wisdom, modesty, chastity, temperance, tolerance, pacifism, etc. It all depends on the vision of your end goal, of the archetype you want to realize or strive for. Maybe your spiritual path is different than the usual, maybe you do not need values like chastity, altruism, charity, and similar. Maybe you do not want to live a life bordering with poverty. In this case again you need money for philosophic idleness in which to develop your spirituality. So, in Nietzsche's terms, some values and practices are more life furthering than others depending on what you want to achieve in the end. You choose your values and principles depending on what fulfills you, what makes your life worth living. If you do not know what this is, you can discover it through philosophic thinking.

Principles are, as mentioned before, rules of behavior or core beliefs. Rules make impulsive behavior into a more deliberate and planned behavior. They direct your actions towards a certain goal. To act impulsively can certainly be more pleasurable, but it makes people forget potentially harmful consequences. Resisting impulsive urges is a part of mental discipline.

Principles are formed by philosophic thinking and argumentation according to your preference. They are tempered by reason and purpose. You decide what you want to achieve and how will you go about doing it. You decide what actions are acceptable or unacceptable and why. When you are unexpectedly faced with a choice to act or not to act, your values and principles represent preformed decisions. You do not have to think it through from the beginning every time, you already decided what you want to achieve beforehand and you act accordingly. This is what it means to uphold your principles.

For example, you have been going regularly to parties late at night for a while. You think about it and decide that it brings you more harm than pleasure. You are tired of alcohol, hangovers, cheap women, and sleeping half of the day. So you decide you will not go to parties any more. Next time someone invites you there is no reason to think about it. You already decided it is counterproductive to your goals so you outright refuse on principle.

A person can have as many reasons to break their principles and ignore their values as there are reasons to form them. But if you do not intend to follow your own ideology there is no point in inventing it in the first place. So, what are the reasons to form and uphold principles?

First of all you made them yourself, so they are not imposed on you. To uphold your own principles is an act of free will and not compulsion, unlike religious principles, for example.

Secondly, you invested certain work and effort into forming the principles. It would be wasteful not to follow them in that case.

Thirdly, assuming that principles you made are backed up by argumentation and reason, it would be irrational not to follow such rules.

And lastly, they are made with a goal in mind. If you do not follow your principles, you will not achieve the goal you intended to achieve. In conclusion, regardless of moral implication of your values and principles, you form them because you want to gain some benefit. If you break your rules, you renounce the benefit you wanted to achieve.

For example, if a person states as a personal principle that they will not tell "white lies", the first chance they are conflicted between upholding their principle and telling a white lie, they may break the principle because it is psychologically easier that way. The purpose of the principle may be to gain more mental strength by facing social awkwardness of telling people what they do not wish to hear. By breaking the principle the person will not achieve the goal, but rather reinforce the weakness they wanted to overcome.

Norms in the society can be highly influenced by religion. It is important to know the doctrine of different religions and their philosophy even if one is not religious. Some people when they have difficulty in life, especially if they are going through some form of existential crisis and/or depression, fall prey to religion. Not all religions are bad, but some of them preach violence. In other cases religious leaders may extort money from the members. The biggest problem with organized religion in general is that it tends to be more political than spiritual, and that spirituality is buried under ceremonies of questionable spiritual meaning and usefulness. In addition, depending on the religion, their doctrine can lean towards dogmatism and indoctrination. Ceremonies certainly can be productive for spiritual development of practitioners, but when they are routinely repeated they can easily become an empty formality. In that case practitioners just do it because it is required, to conform, not because it means something to them. Priests, depending on their religion, sometimes care much more about politics than explaining religious teachings to their followers.

A historical example is fragmentation of Christianity in various factions due to disagreement in doctrine and, more importantly, power, wealth, and influence. Before translation of the Bible to popular language, the masses were completely ignorant of the basis of their religion. They could not explore it on their own, but only believe and follow as they were told by the priests. In the modern times we have all the information at the tip of our fingers. It is no longer necessary to join a religion to learn about it. We can learn about religious doctrines and think about them critically. This allows us to use their philosophy for our benefit without wasting our time and money on potentially useless religious rituals.

Spirituality is important whether you consider yourself

religious or not. Among other human drives, the desire for the transcendent is equally pronounced. Deciding how to deal with it is an important part of developing personal philosophy. Philosophy itself can be used to fulfill the spiritual needs because it deals with metaphysical and existential questions. Besides difficulty in life, another opportunity for existential crisis is when a thinking individual starts to question the core beliefs he or she was raised with. For example, many devout Christians become disappointed with the Church when they compare its doctrine with its practice. They start questioning their religious beliefs and they start moving towards atheism and agnosticism, or they reaffirm their beliefs and move towards being even more devout, sometimes towards fanaticism.

Thus, there are two somewhat extreme paths to take when one is in an existential crisis: to dedicate yourself to religion, or to philosophy. They are extreme only if you go "all out", and this does not have to be something negative if it is tempered by reason. In philosophy one has to question all values presented by the society, redefine all of their own values and principles, and think of new ones if necessary. They have to personally find the answers to their questions and a purpose in life. To do everything alone is certainly harder but in the end it provides freedom and strength of will.

If one dedicates themselves to religion, they get all the answers for granted and they receive help from the community. This path is much easier, but it comes at the cost of freedom of thought. It provides no personal strength because you did not surpass any intellectual obstacles in the process.

Neither of these paths is necessarily better than the other. Some people could not handle the pressure of solitude and absence of god in their life and would be mentally destroyed by it, while others could not tolerate religious life. Which path to choose depends on personal choice, but this book emphasizes the path of philosophy. To develop one's self on this path, a good starting point may be to start reading Platonic dialogues, works by Aristotle, or books on history of philosophy.

History of philosophy offers a brief chronological overview on development of philosophy as a whole and summarized philosophy of individual philosophers. Reading works of individual philosophers offers a better understanding of philosophic topics and thought, but takes much more time for proper study.

Social values can have a strong influence on personal values. Average people just accept them as their own and blindly conform so they can fit in with others more easily. Conformism does not provide a set of consistent principles and values, so people break them when it seems useful to to them. This apparent hypocrisy is natural to humans. Conforming with others may seem rational, but it does not necessarily lead to your wellbeing. People will pressure you to change on a whim, out of jealousy, or if they want to take advantage of you. For example, parents sometimes want to "live through" their children so they pressure them to take certain education or career choice they could not choose themselves. They want to have grandchildren so they pressure their children to marry and have children of their own. It is normal in the society to settle down and start a family at some point. But what if you do not want it? Your married friends and family members, even random people will pressure you and shame you if you say you do not want to live as they do. If your area is predominantly religious, but you do not wish to live a religious life, the community will shame and pressure you into living their way.

As absurd as it may seem, these tactics work very well. Many people sacrifice their self interest and wellbeing to conform with the mainstream society. Some people do not even stop and think if this is the best for them, they just follow as the matter of course.

Conformism limits your potential and curbs critical thinking. Identity of a person is defined by many factors: nationality, race, sex, age, family members, place of origin, political and religious affiliations, etc. None of them a necessarily bad. Some are fixed and unchangeable like those you get at birth like race, family, place of origin, and sex. It is important to take into consideration that you are none of these things. You are not your race, your job, your family, your sexual orientation, your education, your religion, your nationality, etc. It is not bad to take pride in any of these factors, but if you identify with any of them and you have nothing else to it, nothing of your own that defines you as an individual, you will uncritically follow the herd mentality. You will interpret every event and social interaction through the lens of race, sex, politics and similar. Everything will become "sexist, racist, homophobic, and you will have to point it all out". This way of thinking leads to lynch mobs of political activism that perverts justice and criminalizes hurt feelings. As it had been demonstrated thus far in this book, there are great many things in philosophy that can be integral part of your identity, and none of them include these superficial traits. People should judge, and be judged based on their action, meritocracy, and the contents of their character. The point is to take an individualistic approach. If you are related to a group any way, be it by birth, choice, or field of interest, you are not that group. You make your own decisions. You have your own life and goals. You decide what will you become. You do not have to do or think as the group does. You do not have to defend it from criticism. The group is not part of your identity, only your will and actions build your identity.

The reevaluation of social values starts by perceiving social norms as questionable instead of absolute. Customs, tradition, religious prescriptions, and various behavior patterns are intended by social norms, not actions regulated by law. Even though law can be pointless or unjust, it can be very dangerous and unwise to disobey it. So, laws are outside of the scope of this book. If you truly dislike some of your local laws, you can always move to another country. There is nothing else you can do.

It is important to think critically about the values imposed by the society to determine to what degree are they useful and true. Society is made of individuals, and if its norms are not useful for the individual, they will not be useful for the society in general. These norms are mostly defined by tradition and politics. They are unstable and change with every generation. As times change politics can influence your life positively or negatively. As an individual you cannot change any of it, you can only keep track of it and adapt. Political activism is futile. It is not the Stoic way to waste your time on trying to change the unchangeable. You can surpass the societal limitations by reevaluating its values.

Reevaluation of the social values is done by "dissecting" them. It is inspired by Nietzsche's philosophy, but not necessarily done here the way he reevaluated some of the values himself. As mentioned before it is necessary to define them and to observe how they are implemented in society, is that implementation worth the respect, to what degree, and under which conditions. To make this generalized abstract formulation more clear in both theory and practice, one such value will be dissected.

One of the most usual values is respect for elders. The category of elders usually consists of parents, teachers, mentors, and other people who are generally older than us. The reason for which they demand respect is that they are older and more experienced, wiser, and they think we, the younger generations, are somehow in debt to them. This is taken to the extreme in countries heavily influenced by Confucianism, like China or Korea. It is customary in such countries to take the word of elders as "gospel", even when what they say is utter nonsense. To what degree is their claim true true? Parents take care of their children, often much longer than it is necessary. They are supposed to help them form into complete individuals. Why do they have children and do they really give them life? Parents, or people in general, produce children because they want to *have* them. They do not want children, in most cases, for the sake of children, but for the sake of themselves. To satisfy their inborn instincts of reproduction, or to conform with expectations of society. They call this instinct "love". As for them giving life to children, that is something that could be debated. It depends on one's view on how the world functions as a system in general, which is very old and complex

131

question for both philosophy and natural sciences. To answer simply, if children were not born, they would not exist to care about it. Since the children are born, it is the duty of parents to take care of them in every way necessary to the best of their ability. Parents deserve respect only if they do perform their duty to the best of their ability. Abusive and negligent parents along with those who reproduce without restraint while they cannot afford children, deserve no respect.

The same could be said for the teachers and mentors. They deserve respect if they perform their duty adequately. As for people who are older than us, along with their supposedly higher wisdom, they often claim to have built the country for us. Especially war veterans. People fight in wars to protect their *own* country so *they* and *their* loved ones can later live in peace. If the war would start in our lifetime when we can fight, most of us young people would fight for mostly the same reasons of self preservation and preservation of that and those which are dear to us. On the basis of them deserving respect for building the country for us, that does not hold, because people have been doing the same for generations. That is fighting wars and building society from the beginning of human civilization.

People who do not fight in wars, but work in various parts of society mostly do that for personal gain. To earn money, social status, power or something else. It is just to be properly compensated for your hard work, but it is not something exceptional. The work for common good is rare and people who do it for the benefit of the human race deserve respect.

Concerning the higher wisdom of elders, they deserve respect only if they can teach us something. People who spend their life doing mediocre things and achieving mediocre results can hardly teach anyone anything. If they were effective in spreading their immense life experience and wisdom there would be no reason for anyone to write a book like this. Western society would not shift towards Marxism again.

To conclude this dissection of the value of respect for elders, these are the results: the respect for elders is not justified unconditionally but only for those who deserve it. That means one should not respect someone only because that person is older than them, but because that person deserves it due to their characteristics. If the characteristics are unknown, which is the case with strangers, one should be indifferent towards them. Having any attitude, positive or negative, towards people in general, without a just cause, is an irrational prejudice. It is important not to confuse treating people with respect, which is a basic human decency, with the feeling of respect, which is directed to people of exceptional ability or accomplishments.

The reader may or may not agree with the view expressed on

the subject of this particular value, but the concept will serve the purpose of illustrating a way to reevaluate and to examine social values in general. By reflecting this way on other values, one can define them and make them more clear, thus becoming aware of which values to respect, and under what conditions. By devising one's own set of values, he or she will become free of socially imposed values and conditioning for herd mentality. Personal values should be checked and revised along with reasoning behind them. Following blindly any value, belief or principle, even if it is made by one's self, is a dogma. Dogmatic thinking is the death of mental freedom.

Governing principles for one's behavior could be considered personal freedom, necessity, and reason. If one acts within borders of personal freedom, and according to reason, he or she will do no unnecessary actions which will put themselves or others in danger. For example, reckless driving is as dangerous to you as it is to others. It is not reasonable to go out of your way to attack people unprovoked, or to steal or damage their property. Even if you had such tendencies, it is a highly risky business because they will not just let you bully them. In the vast majority of cases you can profit much more from peaceful cooperation than from using force, even if you are a loner. So it is reasonable to refrain from violent acts for sake of self preservation.

Flaws or vices can also be dissected and reevaluated in a similar manner as it is done with values. Not all of them are as bad as they are considered in the society. Some of them might not be bad at all. Attitude towards flaws in general is influenced by social conventions, culture, religion and general behavior of people. All these and any other possible factors influence the general attitude.

Flaw/vice may also be defined as an absence of a virtue. This is similar to the medieval Christian definition of evil, the absence of good. If defined so, flaws seem even more subjective. If a person considers a virtue to be outgoing and social, they may consider the the lack of it to be a flaw, but it is only a matter of preference, not something to be considered a general truth. Another example of subjective flaws/virtues are those established by a religion, like faith and fear of god. A non religious person would consider those two things to be the flaw or something that does not concern them, while a religious person would think the opposite. Such concepts should not be taken seriously as a concrete personality traits but as a relative matter of choice and conviction.

More specific examples of flaws are greed, gluttony, laziness, selfishness, egoism, egocentricity etc. To examine these and any other flaw, it could be considered how useful or harmful they are, and do they affect only an individual in question or others along with the individual.

Greed for unnecessary things, like money for the sake of itself, is certainly irrational and harmful, but greed for knowledge certainly is not. If one is greedy to a point where he or she would do harm to others in order to profit from it, that type of greed affects others and should be avoided.

Selfishness is closely related to greed. Selfishness is equally natural to humans as it is reason. It is useful and vital for survival within reasonable limits. As it was mentioned, society is made of individuals and it can only thrive if people can satisfy each others selfishness through cooperation and agreement. Unreasonable selfishness and greed, like other unrestrained potentially harmful human traits, can easily lead into criminal area. One is free to do what they will, as long as they do not invade the freedom and rights of others. If an individual harms others, they will take action to put a stop to it, or the state itself through law enforcement.

When it comes to traits that damage one's self, it is irrational to hold on to them for long. Being lazy might not be bad from time to time, everyone needs rest after a long hard work, but being lazy all the time is a "sin" against self. Lack of self discipline will cause one to spend their whole life without realizing their potential. If one wants to excel in any activity, there is no room for laziness. Gluttony or alcoholism damage the body, so even from a perspective of a hedonist, it is counterproductive to overdo in these pleasures, because they cause only discomfort in that case.

After the examination of flaw and virtue, it is important to examine the concept of sin. That concept is mainly, if not only, connected to religion, and the most strongly to those big three Abrahamic religions. It is considered to be a sin that which displeases *the God*. How would one know what would displease, as religions describe it, a higher being? It is drawn from ancient, inconsistent texts of questionable origin written by prophets, or people of questionable existence, motives, and sanity. If such texts were really written under inspiration of a higher being they would not become outdated as they are. There certainly is some wisdom to be found in them, but as a whole they are not that impressive.

The proof that sin is something wrong can be taken as evident by the fact of guilty consciousness. Guilty consciousness does not prove anything but the fact that the person is taught to believe that an action is wrong. If a person is taught from birth that, for example, it is a sin to eat yellow fruit. That person would feel guilty for eating such a fruit, even though it may seem absurd that such an action would be wrong. On the other hand, someone may be raised to believe that killing humans for any reason is normal.

Such a person would not feel guilty for committing murder.

One should question and examine all those actions considered wrong by religion and society and determine if it is rational to consider them that way. After the evaluation, in order to gain higher degree of mental freedom, one should free themselves of the dogma imposed by the environment they live in. It may be hard and long work to succeed but it is worth it. There are many ways to be released from the dogma. The first step is to realize the falsity of the dogma, and the next is to do the action repeatedly on purpose, or only when it is necessary until it becomes natural.

Normal is something that is considered acceptable on average. Abnormal is something that is different than the average, be it above or below the average. To be normal means to be average. This abnormality is often considered as a flaw if it is below average, and an object of envy if it is above average. This is the case, for example, with being good at sports, particular school subject, a skill, etc. In an environment with dominating mediocre people, they seek to ostracize or alienate anyone who is out of the norm. That normality is not an objective state of things, but merely a social construct. Thus one should avoid trying to conform to such ideas and resist outside influences.

To reevaluate and set up one's own set of values and principles and behave accordingly means to be different from others. It may be a lonely life, not suitable for everyone. *"To live alone one must be a beast or a god, says Aristotle. Leaving out the third case: one must be both – a philosopher."*⁴⁰ An aim of this book is to provide the tools for one to be able to live alone if they choose so, but as mentioned before, it is up for everyone to decide for themselves what will they do with the knowledge they gain from it.

On reading

Another mentioned way to acquire principles and values is to read mentally stimulating material. Works of philosophy are the best for that purpose because their contents are expressed explicitly and to the point. They deal primarily with certain topics, while fiction focuses on storytelling. But fiction too has its value other than entertainment. It often contains elements of philosophy and it is written in a format that gives a different perspective of the same topic. The format is similar to Platonic dialogues. The conversation between characters creates a different flow of information, and it touches angles of the topic that are usually excluded as redundant in a traditional non-fiction text.

Philosophic elements make fiction more interesting and

---

40 Nietzsche, F., 1972, *Twilight Of The Idols*, The Viking Press, New York, Maxims and arrows 3

realistic. Many of these elements can be contradictory on purpose to show an inner turmoil in a single character, or to make contrast between multiple characters. Just like real people, well written characters should have values, ideals, goals, motivation, and ethics. By observing their behavior we can examine our own. When we see how they deal with various problems it incites us to think how would we do in the same situation. This is an extension to before mentioned philosophic reflection. It is a way to gain new ideas and reevaluate the old ones.

Another useful aspect of well written fiction is the implicit material. The author will implicitly express through metaphor or allegory a part of the contents. He will express values or ideals he may have: courage, friendship, spirituality, altruism, etc. Critique of society in general or contemporary politics, and description of everyday realism is very common throughout literature. The reader may agree or disagree with the author, both in the case of charters and implicit material. In either case the reader is exposed to mentally stimulating material.

Fiction is often a reflection of reality and deals with various problems that people face in real life, but placed in an fictional setting which allows higher degree of objectivity in the reader. It can also be used to distort the perception of reality. This is the case with books and movies used as tools of political propaganda which shows events and nations better or worse than they actually are or have been in the past.

When reading books in general, quality of reading comes before quantity. Some people set up as a goal to read, for example, a hundred books a year. If one can concentrate well, and the contents of chosen books are not too complex, it would not be a problem. However, people start reading for the sake of reading alone, not out of interest for the contents. The quality of that reading method cannot be high. Books must be read with understanding. One may read an entire book, or the mentioned hundred books, without properly understanding the contents of even one of them, which is the same as reading none. Instead of focusing on such goals of quantity, one should focus on the quality of reading without self imposed pressure. So, to draw the most and the best from reading, you should reflect on the contents. This goes double for non-fiction. If you think well about read material, you will understand it better and you may notice something you would otherwise miss. This maximizes the utility of reading and saves time long-term.

A common "trap" of reading instructional literature, i.e. reading about meditation or spiritual practices, is that it gives you a feeling of doing something concrete. It makes you feel like you are being productive while in fact you are hardly doing anything. It is very important to study, but if you do not practice your knowledge it will not produce a real effect. It is important to practice what you learned independently. Experiment and assimilate your knowledge without relying on written material until you feel you have made a progress. After a while go back to your source material and reread it with a "new eyes". You will find new insight and inspiration you could not see before because you lacked the necessary experience.

Concerning the works of philosophers, in most cases they directly describe their point of view, without using stories or different characters. The exception to this concept are works like Plato's dialogues or Thus Spoke Zarathustra by Nietzsche. While reading a work of philosophy it is important to pay attention to the terminology used, definitions of terms and various concepts. Philosophers are educated at that field and their intended audience is also versed in philosophy, so they do not feel the need to explain all the terms. They explain it only if they are inventing a new one or they want to make it clear what they presume under a certain term.

Once the terminology is understood it is possible to understand the work itself. After the bare understanding of what is written, it is important to understand the relations between various concepts and terms, and what do such relations imply. Only once all that is understood, it can be said that the particular work itself is understood. That is what makes philosophy more difficult to read than literature.

Not all of philosophic books are as difficult as it may seem. Western philosophy is based on the ancient Greek philosophy, so most of the authors of that tradition have some fundamental similarities. Knowing the fundamental works of the western philosophy, the works of Plato and Aristotle that is, makes it easier to understand most of it in general. Eastern philosophy has different roots, so someone who grew up in the western part of the world may have difficulty understanding even the basic concepts. Not only the terminology and conception of terms is different but the way it is presented. Despite the fact that eastern and western philosophy are quite different, they share some similarities which can be noticed when they are studied and compared.

Philosophers in their books describe their views on great variety things. Some of them make entire systems which describe their conception of the world in detail. They often begin with metaphysics and/or epistemology which serves as basis for the system. Other philosophers examine individual concepts such as morality, ethics, and what gives the meaning to life while ignoring metaphysics completely. The reader may or may not agree with their views as a whole, but some particular views can be of great use. Their reflection and proposed views on the social concepts, principles, values etc. can incite thinking. If the reader agrees with that particular piece of their work they can adopt it as part of their own viewpoint. If they disagree and can think of objections, they can devise new views on the matter. Another useful method of learning from philosophic or similar material is to be on the lookout for advice and new ideas while reading. These elements can be assimilated for practical use by reflection, understanding, and experience.

The problem with such a way of searching for new ideas is in the fact that people often do not understand fully or correctly the material they are studying. People tend to jump to conclusions and get overly enthusiastic, especially while uncritically reading religious texts. In that case emotions and hope for a better life tend to override reason. There is nothing wrong with being inspired by a written material, but it not good to get carried away by emotions. People are insecure and they often find reassurance in organized religion, and as a consequence they trade reason and common sense for religious dogma.

There are many fake experts and gurus who seek to capitalize on insecurities of others. They adopt various elements from different, often contradictory ideologies which they know only superficially. They latch on particular concepts and expressions like energy, vibration, attraction, chakra, dissolution of ego, etc.

exaggerate their importance, and use them every other sentence as an empty buzzword. This is not an example of true spirituality or genuine interest in religion, but a fleeting fashion trend or virtue signaling, depending on the circumstances and the religion in question. Their intended audience consists of people who have little or no knowledge on religion or philosophy. They desperately need some guidance, so they easily let themselves be exploited.

All theses terms, expressions, or concepts originate from Hinduism. It is a very old religion, and like other old religions it is full of unnecessary mysticism. These people who import foreign ideas like these to the western society make it even more confusing with their superficial understanding.

It is hard to say to what degree they believe their own words, but a lot of them are just trying to sell false hope and wisdom to the naive. This is not directed to people who did proper research and know the material well, but only towards those who superficially study such books or teachings for the purpose of easy profit.

The dissolution of ego, as more experienced people say, is particularly misunderstood concept. Ego should not be destroyed, as some may think. In fact, without ego you are a brain dead shell. Ego is only harmful if identified with outside material things. It is harmful if material things become essential part of your ego, your self image, or personality. This concept is closely connected to what was said before about individualism: you are not your race, community, religion, job, etc. If you want to be free, you must not bind your self worth to outside or irrelevant factors of any kind. Like you are free, so are other people, therefore they cannot be an element that constitutes you as a wholesome person. If you lose a contact with them, i.e. if you break up with a romantic partner, you do not lose a part of yourself. Such event should be accepted with stoic indifference, regardless of the circumstances. Only that way you can continue living your life, instead of developing obsessions like some people do.

Material things like money, a computer, or a car, are just tools. They are not a part of yourself. If your car breaks down, it may be inconvenient, but you are still whole since the car is not a part of your being. It is the way things are, material goods break down and get replaced, while your ego is permanent and unchangeable as long as you live. In Nietzsche's terms, it can be said that ego is the Will to Power. The most fundamental instinct or the drive that moves all others[41]. Indeed, if you strip off all your emotions and thoughts, only ego remains. Ego is the sense of self, self consciousness without which you cannot exist as a person. If you want to be happy, ego or your self-worth must be bound to internal things, like your physical and mental abilities, your

---

41 Nietzsche, F., 2013, *Al di là del bene e del male,* Adelphi, Milano, chap. 2, par. 36

interests, your accomplishments, and similar. It is important to learn how to be satisfied with things that you have, and accept the fact that people you know and tools you own, come and go, while only you yourself are the only constant in your own life. So, enjoy with what you have and with people that make you happy while they are still around. When they leave, and things break down, it does not matter. Nothing essentially changed, you did not lose anything, even though you may feel the loss.

If one wishes to benefit from religious systems, i.e. Buddhism, Hinduism, there is no use focusing only on some ideas that sound nice and are easy to implement while ignoring the rest of the system. Some practices, like meditation, can be used out of context because it is a tool that can be used for various purposes. Concepts such as chakra and energy, however, can only be explained within the context of the system because they may have different meaning depending on the system in which they are examined. To demystify and remove such concepts from their systems of origin for a use free of religious connotations, one must first understand their original use, meaning, and purpose. Only then can they be properly explained to others, or adopted for personal use without making them confusing, incorrect, or useless.

Potential problems are avoided by studying and understanding properly the particular philosophy, or other material of interest. It is absolutely necessary to think critically and to question everything so that you do not become blinded with false conceptions. This is also of utmost importance concerning the organized religion, especially these Abrahamic religions dominant in the west. These religions if followed blindly can make you waste large part of your life on pointless worship and empty ceremonies, instead of using your time for self-improvement.

The aim of this kind of research, as it may already be obvious, is to assimilate useful ideas, concepts, and practices for personal use. Mentioned spiritual posers only conform to the outside appearance. They assimilate appearance only, not useful practices in their essence. Assimilation of concepts and practices is firstly done, as it was mentioned, by proper study and understanding of their original use; secondly one must think of how to implement these concepts or practices for the personal use. For that matter it is important to take into consideration not only the original use and purpose of concepts and practices, but also to abstract their essence to be able to see alternative possibilities.

An example of this process is the use of meditation which will be explained in detail in the next chapter. In essence, to meditate is to perform mental exercises. Originally, its purpose is to reach enlightenment. It is achieved precisely by exercising, or by reaching certain mental states that are necessary for enlightenment. If one does not care about, or does not believe in the idea of enlightenment, how will they assimilate the use of meditation? They will, obviously, take into consideration the essence of that practice, and the essence is to perform mental exercises. For that person the primary goal of meditation is to achieve higher mental abilities, strength, and discipline through mental exercises. This way religious use of meditation becomes irrelevant for the person in question and the practice itself keeps its usefulness and proper use outside the original context.

Solitude is something that fits well with reading. It is not necessary to become completely secluded from others if one does not wish it, but to spend enough time alone to reflect upon that which had been read. Hasty or incomplete analysis of the material caused by unnecessary social distractions will waste a part of potential for learning from the material. Moreover, it is useful to get accustomed to spending time alone in general. People are often afraid of being alone, they tend to do things they dislike and spend time with people they dislike just to avoid loneliness.

Quality time spent with few people you like on rare occasion is much more satisfying than spending a lot of time around uninteresting people. In solitude, if enough time is spent, you loose patterns of behavior absorbed from others, leaving only what is truly yours. In addition, opinions of others lose weight and they no longer have influence on you.

Like it was mentioned before, middle aged and elderly people sometimes say that when alone, they "get all kinds of ideas." They probably get some existential questions, fear of abandonment, illness, and death. Maybe they get some other questions they were supposed to resolve in their youth. To get "all kinds of ideas" is the point of spending time alone and reading books. It is the perfect opportunity to remove mental obstacles and free yourself from artificial boundaries, especially the fear of certain questions.

That is the way to build your own personality, if combined with other techniques mentioned in this book. Excessive sociability, if your character is not strong enough to endure social pressure, breeds only conformism and mediocrity.

On absolutes

There is a tendency in society to put ideas into packages that oppose other packages of ideas. If one person accepts one package they absolutely have to be against the other package. For example if one prefers scientific view on the world, they absolutely have to oppose anything connected to religion. If they prefer one specific political party, they absolutely have to be against everything that says the opposing political party. If they are an atheist, they absolutely have to be against any religious viewpoint. By putting labels on such ideologies ignorant people are appalled, or they bow in awe before the label alone, not the content it represents.

Some of these collections of ideas are made of various elements. It is not wise to discard all of them simply because the label is not to one's liking. This is especially valid for religions because they often contain elements of philosophy which can be of great use if purified from unnecessary worship and groveling. On the mention of meditation, many people would say "that is religion, I do not want to do anything with that" but they would be wrong. Meditation is but a skill that can be employed for religious and non religious purposes.

Modern critics of Christianity, though they do make some valid points, tend to generalize Christianity as religion in general while it is only one particular religion. Based on Christianity alone they tend to say a lot of things about religion in general that is not true in all cases, but only in case of Christianity, and only in those religions that share these particular characteristics.

Many valid points can be made against the Bible as the basis of Christianity, but that is not all there is to it. Christianity certainly had, and still has a great influence on the western society. Its influence is much higher through its philosophical elements than through the conception of the origin of the world. If one wishes to refute Christianity as a whole, it is not enough to refute it only through natural sciences and by refuting the Bible, but also through philosophy.

Many people, though they claim to be against Christian ideas, still retain a large part of its influence in their thought, even some neopagan religious movements such as Wicca, and some forms of theistic Satanism.

When it comes to refuting Christianity on the basis of philosophy, there is no better critic than Nietzsche. But still, he criticized primarily Christianity. It is not possible to extend his critique to all other religions, but only to those that share particular characteristics that were criticized.

Christian apologists mostly defend Christianity based only on the Bible, ignoring the Christian philosophy completely. It is not surprising if it is done by a common believer, but members of the clergy do the same. They make the same mistake as the critics, but from the opposite side of the discussion. Some of religious people of this type take "belief" as something that is a religious monopoly. This opinion can often be encountered in "creationism vs. evolution" discussions. According to that opinion, no one believes in nothing. The argument derived from it is that people who "believe" in evolution are still religious in some sense. From the same argument follows that if you believe in existence of a dishwasher you are religious. This is nothing but absurd sophistry. There is clear difference between religious belief or faith, and epistemic belief which is based on rational reasons and evidence, but it is not yet clear if it is true or not. If a belief is justified and true, then it is called knowledge.

Atheism is not negation of religion but disbelief in existence of god(s). It does not necessarily exclude any viewpoint that can be considered religious, even though the term is primarily used with that meaning in mind. Religion does not imply theism. There are atheistic religions such as Buddhism, Taoism, Confucianism, LaVeyan Satanism etc. Such religions are not based on worship of a deity but offer a philosophy of life with religious elements that can not be empirically proven, but are left to faith. Similarly, an atheist can have religious beliefs while maintaining disbelief in the existence of god(s).

The world is not black and white. The ideas and values which constitute a society are far too complex to be grouped in opposing packages. This absolute way of thinking limits the freedom of thought and leads to dogmatism. People who think like that, whether they are blinded by ideology, tradition, or simply by monotonous closed-minded lifestyle, are closed to new ideas. They will not only discriminate others who think differently for that sole reason, but they will also be closed to possibilities that may improve their life.

To make the best use of ideas, they should be considered not under labels, such as religion and science, but on their truth-likeness and usefulness for life. It is important to know and understand that which one opposes or supports. To know and understand does not imply to accept as true. For example, if one opposes a religion but they know its theory and understand it well, they can still oppose it but with better arguments.

Opposing sides of a discussion may think if the opposition would understand their beliefs they would agree with them. That is because they assume there is an objective truth to it to be understood. However, it does not need to be so in all cases. Lack of understanding often leads to hate and frustration as people desperately attack what they disagree with, focusing only on prejudice, misconceptions, and what little they know on the subject. With knowledge and understanding one can calmly disprove the opposition with reasoning or simply ignore it if it is not worth the trouble.

It may be a good choice to avoid identifying with any type of ideology and adopt only ideas, practices, and values that are useful for life while ignoring everything useless and hindering to your goals. This correlates to what was said before about reevaluation of values and on reading. Identifying with any particular ideology, be it political, philosophic, or religious just unnecessarily limits the freedom of thought and reduces the objectivity of judgment.

Summary

The start towards mental discipline is in the study of philosophy. Philosophy helps you organize your thoughts. It teaches critical and logical thinking, which in turn promote a stable and rational mentality. Such mentality favors objective self criticism and self knowledge which are the basis of self improvement. Through philosophy we question things usually taken for granted, things like values, virtues, principles, social norms, and tradition.

With the help of Stoic philosophy, we can see examples of practical application of philosophy in general. Their teachings promote courage and rational indifference in face of difficulty. By study and understanding of the society and world around us we gain wisdom that will help us achieve our goals. We also learn from the ancient philosophy that excellence and virtue are made by practice and habit, not by birth. On the example of Stoicism we can learn how to shape our mentality: by philosophic reflection we put things in a different perspective which causes moments of "realization". We actively search for these moments by studying different systems of thought philosophic, literary, religious, or otherwise. With the help of moments of realizations we can change our attitude and reinforce our decisions that lead to our wellbeing.

Habits can be hard to break and establish as necessary. Philosophic views may not always be enough to guide the habits, or to deal with negative outside influences. So, to support our decisions we use rationalization and auto-suggestion. Rationalization is used to gauge out advantage and disadvantage, and to switch from emotional thinking to rational thinking. Auto-suggestion is the first active skill that allows you to change your inner state at will.

It is not enough just to follow a pre-formed system, so we develop our own philosophy in solitude. We take inspiration and wisdom from other systems. We adapt them to suit our needs instead of shaping ourselves to fit the system. We purify them from what is useless leaving only the helpful elements. We question authorities and define our own ethical values and principles which are tempered by reason and purpose.

Chapter 2: Meditation as a tool for development of mental discipline

Introduction

Meditation can be defined in multiple ways: a discourse intended to express its author's reflections or to guide others in contemplation[42]; meditation is intense concentration or reflection upon a chosen object; to perform mental exercises.

First definition is sometimes used in texts on philosophy (for example Descartes' Meditations on First Philosophy), and often in medieval philosophy.

In case of Descartes, meditation can be defined as a thought experiment along with the definition of contemplative discourse.

In medieval times meditative contemplation refers to the work of monks and priests who devoted a lot of time and effort in their study and reflection on philosophy and religious texts with intention of combining the two. This was the case in the scholastic period of medieval Christian philosophy. This type of reflection and contemplation in combination with asceticism can have similar effects to meditation as a mental exercise. Asceticism alone without this form of contemplation would be useless for the purpose of mental training.

In modern time, medieval concept of meditative contemplation can be used in combination with reading and meditation as described in this book as a form of mental training, with or

[42] https://www.merriam-webster.com/dictionary/meditation (October/12/2017)

without any form of asceticism. Thought experiments can be used in many ways, for example to dissect and to gain a better understanding of values as described in the previous chapter. Reading the mentioned book by Descartes will certainly give ideas to those interested in the concept.

The second and third definition describe meditation as a skill more accurately. These definitions correspond to eastern conception of meditation which is the primary topic of this chapter. Eastern meditation is not concentration on a concrete topic, but on an object of exercise. This object can be something perceived by physical senses (sound, sensation of breathing, light source), or something in the practitioners mind (visualized image, reciting a mantra). These types of exercises are better for mental training because they directly develop concentration and willpower. Since the training is precise and deliberate it is also fast and effective.

There are as many meditation techniques as there are aims for its use. Meditation is not exclusively religious practice, but a universal skill that can be used by anyone. Regardless of the universal use of meditation, some religions, like Christianity, are against its practice for various reasons. Practitioners of such religions should consider giving up on one or the other.

The same way physical exercises increase physical strength

and ability, meditation increases mental strength and ability. There is no strength without effort and training. Only combination of both mental and physical discipline will make a complete martial artist or a sportsman, for example. Many westerners underestimate meditation and do not take it seriously, or they simply do not have anyone to teach it to them properly, thus limiting their potential in sports, martial arts, and meditation itself.

Skepticism towards meditation in the west is probably caused by its portrayal in pop culture as a futile practice of imagining relaxing natural scenarios or trying to get in sync with vaguely defined cosmic energy. The goal of serious practice of meditation is mental training which can be, depending on the exercise, strenuous rather than relaxing. Relaxation that comes from serious exercise is just a positive side effect, not the primary goal. This book will be of use to people who are interested in serious practice of meditation. The only way to truly understand its benefit is to try it out. In fact, all the teachings about mental discipline expressed in this book started with a sincere desire to try out meditation for one's self.

In this chapter are described basic meditation techniques, application of meditation, its effects, and more. Meditation is of vital importance to expand and further develop the control over emotions gained by philosophic thinking and auto-suggestions alone. In addition, meditation serves to develop greater willpower and control of thoughts that lead towards development of mental discipline.

Basics of meditation

The first and the most important thing for meditation is proper breathing. It is necessary to breathe from the diaphragm. People often use only chest cavity for breathing which does not use the entire capacity of lungs. To determine which type of breathing you use, put a hand on the upper abdomen and check if it is moving. There will be little or no movement in the case of chest breathing. That problem can be solved easily by simple exercises or by consciously changing the breathing method while meditating. It is advisable to use the abdominal breathing permanently because it provides more oxygen so the body gets tired at a slower rate.

If you cannot deliberately switch from chest breathing to abdominal breathing an exercise can be used: lie down on a bed or like surface, and place a hand on your abdomen. The weigh of the hand or the applied light pressure on the abdomen helps to gain the feeling of the diaphragm. Just relax and breathe in as deeply as you can without forcing your lungs and you will notice the difference. If this is not enough to learn the breathing technique, another way is to try moving the hand with one's abdominal muscles while breathing in. It is not necessary to push hard, it serves only to learn the difference between the two methods which makes it easy to continue the practice.

Using abdominal breathing may make you feel lightheaded at the beginning until the body adjusts to higher level of oxygen. Switching to abdominal breathing whenever it crosses your mind will make it a habit and the primary breathing method. Another way to permanently switch to abdominal breathing is to use it in bed before falling asleep. If the exercise is performed in mental state between sleep and wakefulness, it will sink into subconsciousness more easily and will be used automatically. If you notice that you are using abdominal breathing when you wake up, it is a good indication that it is becoming natural.

Sitting properly is next very important thing for effective meditation. The basis for any posture should be maintaining the natural form of the body and sitting upright. It might be the easiest to lie down, but beginners fall asleep very easily, so it is strongly advised against that posture in favor of sitting upright. Upright position reduces the chances of falling asleep during meditation. For effective meditation it is not necessary to learn a large variety of positions usually associated with yoga. Just one or two natural positions will suffice. Sitting on a chair with back straight and shoulders relaxed without leaning back is one of the simplest positions to use for meditation. Pull your feet under the chair and rest your hands on your thighs. Strive to balance your weight evenly to increase the quality of meditation. If you lean too much forward or backwards it will put more strain on your back or abdominal muscles which causes discomfort and restricts your breathing. At the beginning, it can be easier to find the suitable form before meditation with your eyes open.

It is important not to lean back because it restricts proper breathing. This posture does not require high body flexibility as some other postures do. If one would set up the back of the chair so they can lean back and relax, it would be easy to fall asleep like if they were lying down, so it is best to avoid it.

Another common position is to sit on the floor with legs crossed. In this case it is advisable to sit on something like a cushion. It is easier to keep the back straight that way. In the both first and the second position, it may be hard at first to maintain proper posture because back muscles get tired as they are not used to that type of work. The problem will gradually disappear with regular practice. People who do regular back exercises will be able to sit properly without difficulty.

Keeping the back straight is vital because sitting in an awkward position for long time can cause back pain and spine deformation. Uncomfortable and improper posture is not only unhealthy but also distracting. It poses even a bigger problem for beginners because the discomfort arises just as they start getting into meditative state. It is important to persist in regular exercise without straining yourself until your body adjusts to it.

While meditating it is also important to move as little as possible (ideally be completely still) and to keep the eyes closed at all times unless the exercise requires otherwise. Sudden moves or opening the eyes will interrupt the meditative state. Because of the physical inactivity and closed eyes it is easy to fall asleep, which also interrupts the progress and the session can be considered a failed attempt. When you gain enough experience in meditation and can maintain mental focus, that focus alone will keep you awake. At this level it is possible to meditate while lying down, or late at night. Before that, as a beginner, you may fall asleep even while sitting.

To prevent falling asleep, performing light exercises or washing the face with cold water beforehand will make you feel more awake. If you become tired and sleepy, you should stop the exercise and continue later when you see fit. You should also avoid doing meditation exercises late at night or just after you wake up because it may be easier to fall asleep at that time too.

Concerning the time of the day for meditation, it is the best to choose according to personal biorhythm. There is no general rule, some people are naturally able to concentrate better at different time of the day so they should determine what is the best for them accordingly.

Being impatient and anxious to get results during meditation will also interrupt the progress because it draws attention from the exercise. To avoid this problem it is the best to relax and focus on the present moment. Forget about your past or future worries. Whatever problem you may have to solve, it can wait for 10-15 minutes. Move your awareness to your senses and feel your surroundings for a few seconds. That is a good trick to draw your attention from everyday events to the present so you can calmly continue the exercise. However, for effective meditation it is best to maintain your awareness inside your body. Observe the changes in your inner state and the state itself. This causes deeper meditation and reduces the interruptions from your senses.

With proper meditation, higher concentration and calmer mind will manifest within first few sessions. Proficiency in the chosen exercise will slowly increase with every session and will become noticeable within few weeks, depending on the frequency of practice.

During meditation senses become sharper and any sudden noise may feel painful like an electric shock. To avoid that and other interruptions, it is the best to choose as peaceful and as quiet place as one can find. Interruptions reduce quality of the meditation session and increase the overall time you will need to master the chosen technique, or grasp the basics at the beginning. One properly performed exercise that does not last a long time will be of much more use than an exercise drawn out for an hour, but frequently interrupted. If one is unable to find a peaceful place for meditation, distractions can be considered an additional element of training. It will surely be more difficult to begin in such conditions, but surpassing the obstacle will make the practitioner more proficient at meditation.

Distractions will have much higher effect on someone if they let these distractions annoy them. It is important to accept them as they are, with indifference. This way they will be much easier to ignore if they are not too intense. Monotonous sounds of traffic, talking people, or even construction can be easy to ignore if you do not focus on them.

Meditating at least once on subsequent days produces better results than meditating every once in a while. Just like tiredness accumulates in the body with everyday exercises, mental strain accumulates with frequent meditation, especially when advanced exercises are performed. However, exercises like vacant mind do not cause strain, but reduce it instead. Meditating more than once a day also produces good results, but every next meditation exercise becomes more and more tiring and mentally demanding. When you are skilled enough you can meditate multiple times a day without a problem. If you want to train hard, rest between the exercises long enough for your mind to recover from strain and alternate between strenuous and non strenuous exercises.

Concerning the duration of every exercise, it is not necessary to measure the exact time spent. A session should last as long as the practitioner is not too tired or has not lost the focus. In the following described exercises there is a recommended duration for each exercise. That is only a rough estimate of time spent meditating to gain significant benefit from the exercise. When performing advanced exercises, the approximate duration is used to keep track of the progress.

The estimate of the duration can be made by measuring the time from start to finish of the exercise by a stopwatch, or by comparing the starting and ending time on a clock. The exact time would be hard or impossible to determine because it takes a few minutes to achieve the meditative state of mind. Practitioner can always extend the duration of the exercise if they can maintain the focus. Extended meditation is highly beneficial if done properly as it leads to higher mental discipline.

If you have a little time, about 5-30 minutes for meditation, you can use an application on your phone to countdown the chosen duration of the practice. This way you do not have to worry about being late, only about the exercise. Applications made for timed physical exercises can be useful in this case. The disadvantage of countdown meditation session is that you may be disturbed from a deep meditation at the end of countdown. Along with not having to worry about time spent meditating, an advantage to this method is that you can break down meditation session into shorter periods, each with a different meditation technique. This can be useful to "freshen up" your focus and keep it to a maximum.

Basic meditation techniques

To repeat once again, meditation should be as effortless as possible. Despite the intense focus of the exercise, you should strive to relax both mentally and physically. Do not force the change in your mind, but let it happen naturally. Avoid straining your mind. It will just tire you out without any benefit. Do not hurry for results or think about what will you do after the exercise. Instead, immerse yourself in meditation. Just focus on doing the exercise properly and results will follow spontaneously. Along these lines Bardon[43] advises regular, systematic, quality

---

43   Bardon, F., 2018, *"Initiation Into Hermetics"*, Merkur Publishing, USA, p. 60

practice instead of pushing yourself hard. However, some people like Peter Carroll[44] advise "inhuman effort" in meditation exercises. They are probably both right under the right circumstances. When you notice you are stagnating after a long period of regular training. It becomes a routine and your focus gradually weakens. In that case it is beneficial to invest a hard effort to break through the routine and laziness. When you get back on the track continue with moderate exercise.

The origin of these techniques is probably Buddhist or Hindu, but their interpretation and application as described here are the author's. They can be found On-Line on various pages which deal with topics on these religions, and in books such as Peter Carroll's *"Liber Null"* and Franz Bardon's *"Initiation Into Hermetics"*.

The train of thoughts[45]:

Following the above mentioned instructions, sit in a comfortable position, close your eyes, breathe deeply from the diaphragm, and observe the thoughts that come into your mind. It is not necessary to think actively about them, just observe

---

44 Carroll, P., 1987, *Liber Null*, Weiser Books, San Francisco, p. 16
45 Bardon, F., 2018, *"Initiation Into Hermetics"*, Merkur Publishing, USA, p. 66

passively as they appear and disappear. While doing so, it is important to pursue the train of thoughts attentively without losing yourself like you are about to fall asleep, or by actively thinking about the thoughts that come to your mind. If you start feeling tired, it is the best to stop the exercise before sleepiness overcomes you.

This exercise should be relatively easy for everyone. It serves to familiarize one's self with meditation and to achieve beginning level of focus necessary to perform other, more effective techniques. This exercise should be done for 5-10 min every day, or at least as often as possible if one is busy, until they are able to perform it without getting tired or sleepy and without losing the train of thoughts.

Thinking actively about a problem or event that one may have encountered in everyday life means losing the train of thoughts and passive observation. In that case simply return to passively observing state of mind and continue the exercise.

As one becomes more proficient in this exercise they will notice that thoughts gradually become less chaotic and become more and more focused until only few remain. This exercise can be used as a beginning step in preparation for exercises of complete vacancy of mind. The next step towards that particular exercise or technique is the breathing exercise which will be described later.

Once this exercise is done properly for 5-10 min, and the practitioner feels confident, they may proceed to the next, more advanced exercise. People who do a lot of mental work, like studying, may have this technique already covered.

Basic visualization techniques

Sit in a comfortable position, relax, close your eyes, breathe deeply and properly as described before. Take a little time to adjust to the sitting position and for your thoughts to stabilize like in the previous exercise. Maintain proper posture, breathing, and eyes closed during the entire exercise. Move as little as possible. Moving excessively or opening your eyes during meditation will cancel most of its effects and you will have to start from the beginning to restore the acquired mental state. When ready start one of the following visualization exercises:

White ball visualization[46]: imagine a white ball in a black space. Maintain the visualization of the ball in your mind while blocking off all other thoughts. If the concentration is broken and thoughts wander off to unrelated matters, return the focus to the ball. After some time during the exercise, when you start losing

---

46 A Buddhist technique, along with *"Flame visualization"*

the focus, imagine moving into the ball, where there is another white ball in the black space. Repeat the process until you get tired or unable to maintain concentration.

Try to feel more relaxed and focused on every repetition. This change from one ball to another can help extend the exercise as it may be difficult at first, to maintain a static mental image for extended period of time.

The visualization does not have to be perfect and it can be hard to maintain at the beginning. It will become better and easier with practice. It should be performed 5-15 min per session. It is advisable to perform it at least once on 3 consecutive days for the most benefit.

Flame visualization: imagine a flame of any color, its dynamic movement with or without the sound it produces. Maintain its image in the mind while discarding all thoughts unrelated to the exercise. If your mind wanders off, return it to the visualization of the flame. After some time, when your focus is increased, imagine yourself engulfed in the aura of that flame and maintain the visualization for a while. After that imagine the flame spreading to the room you are in, then the next room and slowly the entire building, and the world in the end.

The expanding of the fire serves the same purpose as changing the ball in the previous exercise. On the every step try to feel more relaxed and focused. Maintain the visualization to the best of your abilities. Stop the exercises if you feel tired or sleepy. The exercise should be performed for 5-15 min per session at least once on 3 consecutive days for the best effect.

These simple visualization techniques, or exercises, serve to develop further what was achieved in the train of thoughts exercise. They are somewhat more difficult than the first exercise, the train of thoughts, as they require higher concentration and more of mental effort to perform adequately. This is precisely why their frequent practice increases willpower and concentration. Neither the visualization nor the concentration have to be perfect at this point. The main goal is to gain experience, improve mental abilities and get a better understanding of the practice of meditation.

One should not proceed to more complex basic techniques before gaining enough skill and experience in these simpler techniques because they will be too hard to perform properly. People who find visualization in general too difficult may use the breathing exercise from the advanced techniques, but under an easier criterion.

Sound reproduction[47]: Similar to visualization technique

---

47 Inspired by techniques mentioned by Bardon in *"Initiation Into*

where you produce an image in your mind, in this exercise you produce a sound in your mind. This exercise can be of use to those who find visualization too difficult.

The principle is the same as that in the visualization exercise: maintain focus on the sound while blocking out any thoughts unrelated to the exercise. The effects should be the same as with the previous exercises.

The chosen sound should be something simple that can be reproduced indefinitely, like hum of an engine, buzz of a bee, purring of a cat, repeating music sample, etc. More complex sounds like dynamic music or voices might be unsuitable for starters as they are irregular and cannot produce the same effect as continuous monotonous sound.

Sensory meditation

In sensory meditation exercises, you focus on an actual sound or an object instead of reproducing it in your mind. In some religions, like Buddhism and Hinduism, practitioners focus on sounds of bells while meditating or watching a candle flame in a dark room.

The exercise can be performed in many ways. There is no need to buy recordings of special "meditation music" or buying special

Hermetics"

candles. If you have a fan in your computer loud enough to be heard, but not too loud to be distracting, it can serve for meditation practice. The procedure is the same as before: close your eyes, sit in a comfortable posture, breathe properly, and focus on the sound of the fan while blocking out any unnecessary thoughts. Do not analyze the quality of the sound, just observe it passively. Any other similar monotonous sound can be used for this purpose like rain, sound recordings etc.

Similarly, any music that is not too chaotic can be used for meditation if the particular piece is not too short. It should last at least 10 minutes for a quality meditation session. If it is too short, your meditation will be interrupted when it ends. Music containing long repeating segments can be of great use for this type of meditation. If you do not already have any such music you can find a free program and assemble it from prerecorded samples, or compose and record it yourself if you play an instrument.

Concerning the mentioned visual meditation by focusing on a flame of a candle, any small light source will do. If you cannot or will not use a candle, you can use a small LED light. They can be find almost on any electrical device such as keyboards, monitors, TVs, speakers etc., where they serve as power indicators. Darkened room serves to hide other objects so they do not draw attention.

These visual exercises can be a good preparation for visualization exercises, but they also might be straining for the eyes so other mentioned techniques are a good alternative. Another point to take in consideration is that it is easier to achieve deeper meditation state with closed eyes, especially at the beginning. At the end it might be just a matter of preference.

Mantra

In this type of meditation you focus on repeating a series of words instead of visualizing an object. Words can be anything. For example, in Hinduism they use names of deities in mantras. Some Buddhist schools recite prayers over and over. In Surat Shabd yoga it is advised that you choose words that move your focus inwards, into the mind, as opposed to outwards, out of your body. Such words can be any internal mental concept. For example intuition, concentration, cognition, meditation, knowledge, wisdom, freedom, etc. It does not really matter what you choose, the only important thing is that you fully focus on these words during meditation. You do not repeat them mechanically without thinking, but your pause and acknowledge every word in your mind. You are fully conscious of the process and you pay attention to every word. As you switch from one word to another your mind is focused on the process like it would be focused on a visualization, and thus it blocks out all unrelated thoughts causing the same meditative effect. The switching between words is more dynamic than visualizations or sound reproduction so it may be useful for both beginners and more experienced practitioners.

Movement meditation

Movement meditation exercises can be done effectively when the basics of meditation are practiced long enough so that practitioner can easily focus on the act of moving and ignore unnecessary thoughts. In the previous exercises it is required to keep still because any sudden movement interrupts the meditation. In this type of exercise concentration is directed on the movement itself, rather than on a visualization or other object of focus. The movement cannot be chaotic but monotonous, it must be done slowly with attention and focus.

In Zen Buddhism it is recommended to do any action, any everyday activity, with maximum attention. Thus you improve the quality of your work and you exercise mentally in the process. This concept can be useful for everyone. If it is too hard to maintain the concentration all the time, fully focusing only on important tasks can greatly increase their effectiveness and quality.

A concrete exercise of this type is to focus on your feet while you walk. Relax like in other exercises and move at your natural pace. With every step pay attention to the sensation of touch at the bottom of your feet. Keep the focus on the sensation and disregard everything else. This exercises very quickly produces meditative state. Its greatest advantage is that it can be practiced virtually anywhere, especially if you like taking walks.

Movement meditation is specially useful while doing physical exercises because it helps to prolong the training. Usually when people exercise, they tend to focus on how tired they are getting, they want to get it done quickly, or they do not feel like exercising which causes them to get tired faster and stop the exercise. If you focus on the exercise instead and block any distracting thoughts you will work longer and harder because it prevents the auto-sabotaging mental process.

For example if you are doing push-ups, focus on the action, maintaining proper form, and counting of every push-up you do. If you are practicing martial art techniques, focus on every strike or block you perform. This way the action becomes the object of meditation, just like a visualization in previous exercises.

To make the physical exercise into a more effective mental

exercise, physical activity should not be too hard, which depends on your physical condition. In that case you would become tired before a significant mental exercise is done. If the physical activity is light or medium in intensity and monotonous in rhythm, it can be extended to at least 10 minutes which makes it a good meditation session.

Movement meditation does not allow the same depth of meditation as stationary exercises do, but it is still a very useful technique because it helps to extend the use of mental discipline in everyday life and it reduces the dependency on the stationary meditation. The principles are always the same. As you practice on the move you will learn how to use aspects of meditation without having to stay still.

Advanced basic techniques

These techniques are not necessary to develop emotion control by self-hypnosis, which will be described later, but they are necessary to reach the higher level of mental discipline and emotion control which surpasses basic self-hypnosis. They can take months of training before mastering one of them, even when one is experienced in meditation. Because of their difficulty it is advised to leave them for later (with exception of the breathing exercise which can be very useful at beginners level) after self-hypnosis and other techniques are learned.

There are even more complex techniques which are truly advanced. That is why these can be called *basic*, as they serve as preparation for much more difficult techniques. These techniques are not necessary for this manual so they will not be described, but if the reader is interested in them, they can be found in various other books.

Breathing exercise[48]: sit in a comfortable position, close your eyes, relax and breathe deeply like in previous exercises. Count deep breaths and discard all thoughts other than counting. Do not force deep breathing but let the air flow naturally. Every time your thoughts wander off restart the counting. At first, the aim is to count to 10 without thoughts wandering off. As you get better, the aim is set higher. Once you can count breaths for about 10 minutes without losing count or thoughts wandering off the slightest, the exercise can be considered mastered. At the beginning it is not necessary to be too strict with yourself regarding the restarting of the process, but as you progress it must be done firmly, or there will be no improvement.

48 A Buddhist technique, also mentioned by Bardon in *"Initiation Into Hermetics"* and by Peter Carroll in *"Liber Null"*

To keep track of the progress, a string of beads can be used to count errors while meditating so that you do not lose focus on that side activity. There is no need to buy a string of beads, just take a spare shoelace and tie a few groups of knots on it. Organize the groups and their corresponding number of knots depending on your preference. The string does not have to be anything fancy because it is a tool, not a fashion accessory or an object of worship.

To measure time, you can use a stopwatch to determine how long was the meditation session, or calculate how many breaths you can do in 10 minutes and set it up as a goal. It might seem ridiculous, but during meditation as breathing gets deeper and slower, it may take 6-10 seconds to complete a breathe in and out cycle which you count as 1 breath during this exercise.

When performed properly, this exercise brings the mind very close to a vacant state so it is a second step before practicing complete vacancy of mind. At the beginners level, breathing exercises can be a very useful tool for inducing trance state which will be explained later in this book. Furthermore, it does not rely on visualizations so it can be of use to those who have trouble with them. Such people can use this exercise instead of visualization techniques by focusing on the sensation of breathing. Instead of counting for 10 minutes flawlessly, beginners can try counting at least to 10 or as much as they can without losing the count. They need not do it rigorously without mistake as it is too difficult at beginners level.

Similarly to movement meditation, this exercise can also be used to reduce dependency on stationary meditation. Once you are skilled enough you can quickly regain concentration and clear your mind by taking a deep breath and focusing on that action.

Shape visualization[49]: imagine a simple geometric shape like circle, triangle, rectangle, or anything similar and keep its image in your mind. At the beginning the image is hard to maintain and it is not clear, so you should focus on its vague outline until it becomes precise. Once you are able to maintain the clear image for 10 minutes without any interruption, the exercise can be considered mastered.

This exercise is very similar to basic visualization exercises. The main difference is in the criteria and the goal. The basic exercises are used only to gain basic experience, willpower, concentration, and visualization skills. It is not necessary to keep the image perfect and without interruptions for long time. Shape visualization may be more difficult to perform because these simple shapes are more detailed than a ball or a flame. If the same criterion of maintaining the perfect visualization for 10 minutes

---

49 A technique mentioned by Carroll in *"Liber Null"*

would be applied to the basic visualization techniques, they would also become advanced.

Shape visualization exercise serves to develop mental abilities further from what was learned before. Practicing it consistently and seriously will yield drastic improvement of the basics, thus preparing the practitioner for more advanced techniques.

Vacant mind[50]: in this exercise it is necessary to maintain complete vacancy of mind for 10 minutes without interruptions. Mastering the breathing exercise will make this one easier. Average people often say that it is impossible to "think about nothing" and when you think you are doing it, you are actually thinking about not thinking. This statement is false and it is made by people who have little or no mental training or discipline. Everyone, with a little effort, can maintain vacancy of mind for a few seconds. Maintaining it for longer periods of time, however, takes training. In the state of vacant mind remain only awareness or consciousness. It does not matter if your senses pick up data as long as you do not actively monitor it or process it with your mind. As the exercise progresses and the practitioner becomes more focused and absorbed in the process, they will ignore even the sense data. Like with other mediation exercises it helps to

---

50 Technique mentioned by Bardon in *"Initiation Into Hermetics"* and by Carroll in *"Liber Null"*

keep your attention inside your body. Stay as still as possible. Concentrate on your breathing and the changes in the inner state caused by meditation. Imagine there is nothing outside you, there is only you. If your attention moves to sense data or thoughts, remind yourself there is nothing outside and clear your mind again.

More experienced people say the key to achieving vacant mind state is in relaxing your tongue and eyes. Whenever you think of something, your tongue will subconsciously twitch like you are talking, and your eyes will focus as if you are looking at the imagined object. So, instead of fighting the thoughts themselves, an easier method is to focus primarily on your tongue and relax it. In addition, relax your eyes and let them go out of focus to achieve a "parallel look". Which means, each eye is directed straight forward, like you are looking far away in the distance.

All these meditation techniques are just examples of various existing techniques. They can all be modified according to personal preference. Other similar techniques can be found elsewhere or invented by experimentation or imagination. That which makes these techniques useful and effective is focusing on a single object, which helps one discipline their thoughts to flow according to their will rather than letting them form chaotically according to given situation. All that is part of gaining mental discipline and subordinating thoughts and emotions to the mind, which will be described more accurately later in this book. There are other methods and purposes of meditation that can be found in other systems, but they will not be described here as they are not important for the topic discussed in this book.

For a successful meditation, it is important to maintain proper body posture, breathe deeply without forcing it, move as little as possible (ideally remain completely still), relax mentally and physically, keep your attention on the inside, and to keep your eyes closed if required by the exercise. At the beginning it might be difficult to remain focused or even awake. To reduce the problem it is the best to choose time when one feels the most awake and focused, and place where they will be undisturbed during the meditation. One should not get discouraged or frustrated if they fail. Persistence and hard work will be rewarded with success and resulting self-improvement.

Another important thing to keep in mind is that meditation techniques may not be equally effective for everyone. It is not necessary to perform the exercise exactly the way it is described if it does not work after a while. All exercises can be changed to a degree to fit personal preferences as long as it does not defeat the purpose of the exercise. An ineffective exercise can also be substituted with another that will yield the same result. One will also learn by experience simple tricks which will help them perform a difficult exercise more effectively and easily. It would be useless to describe all these details because they are all a matter of individual preference. If one would keep in mind all the detailed instructions during the exercise it would only distract them from performing it properly.

State of trance

Trance can be defined as any altered state of mind. In dictionaries, trance is defined as complete or partial lack of subject's consciousness of their surroundings, as a dreamlike state, as a half conscious state, and as a state of mental absorption in an activity. The accuracy of these definitions depends on the depth of the trance. Only the deepest possible trances cause lack of awareness of one's surroundings. It may sound intimidating if one is unfamiliar with that mental state, but once understood it will not seem as such. This definition, however, does not apply to meditation. It is the goal and highly desirable to achieve the depth of meditation where you can effectively forget about your surroundings, but you will be easily roused from that state by a sudden external stimuli. In the definition of a trance it is intended that it is not possible to end it by a stimuli, which is true in extreme cases.

That which causes partial or complete lack of sensory awareness of subject's surroundings is his or hers intense concentration on that what they are doing in their mind. That state can be dangerous if induced unwillingly by chemical abuse because the subject can not react to their environment and can get hurt or killed by accident. If it is induced willingly, by using a safe method, there is no danger whatsoever because it can be interrupted at will.

An example of a light trance is daydreaming. In that state a subject is focused on their imagination and may be unaware of what is happening around them. If the subject is called by a friend, they might not hear them unless the friend shouts, or physically shakes them. The same may happen if someone gets absorbed in reading or watching TV.

An example of deep trance is when a religious zealot in deep prayer or after a religious ritual does not respond to outside influences, feels no pain if injured, and similar phenomena. Such states can also be induced, as mentioned before, by chemical abuse or other means.

These examples were explanation of the dictionary definition and conception of the trance by the average people. What follows is the definition of a trance as an altered state of mind. The state of mind is altered from that which is normally present when one does no extraordinary things, when one feels completely "normal". Every alteration of the "normal" state of mind could be called a trance. Mild trances occur spontaneously when someone concentrates and gets absorbed into some of their activities, which is mentioned in some dictionaries as an example. In that case they exhibit behavior similar to that of daydreaming. When a person is skilled enough they can ignore anything that distracts them from their current activity, or induce a state of heightened awareness, which does not fit the dictionary definition of a trance as lack of awareness or consciousness of surroundings. Those both states are not the usual mental state, thus they can be called altered state of mind and as such a trance.

Some people, like professional sportsmen or martial artists, learn to use similar states naturally with long training. They call this state to be in "the zone". Some benefits of trance in their case is increased focus and slightly dulled feeling of pain and tiredness which help them improve their performance. To exploit the state of trance fully, one must be able to induce it at will. To do so, one must know the principles behind it.

There are many ways to induce a trance, and the simplest and the safest is meditation. If one has practiced before mentioned exercises or some other meditation techniques, they may have already noticed changes in mental state during the practice. First step in learning how to induce a trance is to recognize the change from normal mental state into a trance. It is counterproductive to describe how does that feel, because it varies between individuals. People would try to "find" that exact described feeling while meditating, thus their mind would become analytically overactive which sabotages the attempt to induce the trance. For that reason it is the best for everyone to learn to notice the subtle change between the mental states by personal experience. The easiest way to learn this is by meditating while monitoring one's own mental state. It is vital, as mentioned before, not to think analytically because that interrupts the trance, but observe passively what goes on in the mind instead.

Inducing the state of trance

After defining the state of trance, it is appropriate to explain how to induce it. If the reader has practiced any of the mentioned, or other similar exercises, they may have noticed that meditation if done properly, inevitably leads to a state of trance.

There are a few conditions that highly influence induction of a trance. For beginners the most important factors to achieve that are: to relax and to be motionless. Take time until thoughts become focused, concentrate on your breathing, and perform the exercise. If one gets anxious and tries too hard they will not be able to induce the trance. Waiting for thoughts to stabilize will help one become focused enough to maintain concentration on the breathing or a visualization. Such a way of focusing on a single concept, be that act of breathing or the visualized object, causes the change from usual active and chaotic state of mind into more focused, altered state of mind or consciousness – a trance.

Maintaining as perfect motionlessness as possible causes the practitioner to be significantly more absorbed into their introspection. It draws attention from the outside to the inside and helps to shut off the distractions.

By practicing this process one will learn how to induce a trance willingly by meditation as well as principles behind it.

More experienced and skilled individual can skip a few steps of the process by emptying their mind, focusing on breathing, and simply willing to change their mental state. They will induce the trance in seconds if not instantly. This method is not suitable for beginners as they do not have the necessary mental discipline to use it, but they can develop it in relatively short time if they practice frequently and seriously.

The benefit of the trance state is in the fact that is allows one to access their subconsciousness. By performing meditation exercises over a long period of time, one becomes gradually aware of layers of subconsciousness. This awareness causes unique ability of introspection, hard if not impossible to achieve otherwise.

Access to subconsciousness may cause fear in average people. They expect to find there something that will make them behave in an unexpected and harmful way, which is another irrational misconception. One does not need the access to their subconsciousness in order to be influenced or even controlled by it. If what they believe was true, they would behave in that manner regardless of their knowledge of the contents of their subconscious part of mind. In fact, the largest part of human mind consists of subconsciousness. It shapes your thoughts and emotions without your knowledge, and thus it controls your actions. Whenever you decide to change your bad habits, it is subconsciousness that produces the urges that make it difficult to succeed.

Becoming aware of the contents of subconsciousness will allow one to learn more about themselves, their motivation, instincts, emotions, desires and other factors that influence their behavior and change it as they see fit. This might be one of the greatest long term benefits of meditation. However, it is important to keep in mind that most of the subconsciousness will remain hidden.

Subconscious can be influenced favorably through auto-suggestion mentioned in the first chapter and self-hypnosis which will be explained next. This relates back to what was said about being honest with yourself as opposed to self-deception. If you keep convincing yourself that you are better or worse than you are, if you have negative thoughts about yourself, or if you deny your flaws, it all has similar effects to influencing your subconsciousness through meditation. The difference is that meditation practice causes deeper and faster changes. The concept of self-knowledge and being honest to yourself as mentioned in the first chapter serves to gradually purify your subconsciousness and fill it with positive and true thoughts that will promote mental health and development. It also serves to get used to observing your faults objectively so that you can change for the sake of yourself and your wellbeing. So, for that same reason, it is very important to keep a positive objective attitude in general. As it was mentioned before, if you make a mistake, it is counterproductive to dwell on it and demean yourself about it. Instead you should work on fixing it and avoid repeating it in the future. This positive and rational attitude should be taken into consideration when using self-hypnosis to achieve your goals. This practice will not cause problems if you do not do it properly short-term, but long term it will. Just like you develop complexes and insecurities from negative attitude in normal thought process, you will do the same with poor use of self-hypnosis.

Self-hypnosis

Now that the basics of the trance have been explained, it is possible to describe some of its practical applications. One of the most useful applications of trance state for the control and manipulation of one's own emotions is self-hypnosis. It is used by imprinting auto-suggestions into their subconsciousness, thus greatly increasing the effectiveness of suggestions. Self-hypnosis used this way can be considered an upgrade, or a more advanced form of auto-suggestion. It can be used not only for control of emotions but also for changing personality and habits more effectively.

The difference between hypnosis and self-hypnosis is, obviously, in the fact that hypnosis is performed on others, possibly without their knowledge or consent, while self-hypnosis is performed on self with self-interest in mind. Learning to perform self-hypnosis and the principles that govern it will help one recognize when such techniques are used on them and to negate the effects.

To use self-hypnosis for the purpose of controlling emotions, induce a state of trance by meditation. When relaxed and focused in the process, use an auto-suggestion like: emotions off, there is no emotion, or something similar. Repeat the phrase in your mind and try to understand the idea. Understanding the idea will make the phrase more than just words. In the process try to feel yourself becoming calm and peaceful while the emotions are fading. This following thought or sensation after the auto-suggestion will reinforce the intention to achieve the goal of turning off the emotions. This step is necessary if one wishes to learn how to freely influence their emotions. It is not as simple as it may seem, and it is not permanent. This practice is reversible and easily undone at early stages so it can be safely experimented with. If the reader is not interested in drastic changes to emotions, they can still use this process without worry as they will be able to modify it to suit their needs when they are skilled enough.

The origin or the exact form of the proposition used as auto-suggestion does not matter. What does matter is the intention and that the used line can be associated with the intention. Using a line that has strong mental impact on the user, a line which can be considered inspiring, will greatly increase the effectiveness of the process. Repeating the same procedure will increase the intensity and the duration of the effects. If an unimpressive line is used, it may take a bit more time and repetition to achieve the same result as with an inspiring line. Using the same proposition, or the same auto-suggestion, for the same purpose will make it more effective and easier to use. For that purpose it would be the best to use the same one at least until the user has become proficient in the use of the technique. With experience and skill there are other methods that can be employed for various other purposes which will be explained later.

Archetypes

Archetypes can be used to make it easier to understand the concept of self-hypnosis. The term can be found in many different areas like literature, philosophy, psychology etc. The topic was mentioned and partially explained in the first chapter. Definitions of the term archetype that can be of use for this book are: the original pattern or model of which all things of the same type are representations or copies; an idea or mode of thought.[51]

The archetype, serves to give you an idea of what you want to achieve which makes it easier to focus your effort towards a single goal. Archetypes are made through thousands of years of religion, culture, and education which makes them a powerful force. If you learn how to tap into them they can be an invaluable tool to shift your mental development in a desired direction.

Archetype can be something like a warrior, Stoic Sage, a soldier, a god, an exceptional person, a character from a game or literature, an animal, a religious figure etc. Every one of them has

51 https://www.merriam-webster.com/dictionary/archetype (October/20/2017)

its own set of characteristics and ideas that can be used to inspire yourself. For example, a warrior is someone strong in body and spirit, courageous, and skilled in battle. To use the archetype of warrior for self improvement one just needs to imitate the model.

What does one need to do in order to be skilled, courageous, and strong in body and spirit? He needs to do general physical training and martial arts training for the strength of body and martial skill. For the strength of spirit and courage, for example, he needs to face his fears and difficulties in life as well as people who want to bully them.

To use an archetype for self-hypnosis one must make themselves inspired by it. Choose an archetype or more of them that fit the goal and say to yourself, for example "I am a warrior" or "I will become a warrior". Think of the characteristics associated the their archetype and imagine them as your own. Imagine yourself to be and to look like a warrior you want to be. You do not necessarily need to want to become like the chosen archetype, but the goal is to be inspired to work to achieve a result. In this case to be strong, skilled, and brave. You use that intention and inspiration to set up an ideal for continuous motivation which helps fight laziness and procrastination. Once the ideal is set up you just have to keep it in mind to motivate yourself to keep working on it regularly. Once you establish good habits of regular exercise, archetype will no longer be necessary until you start succumbing to laziness again. At that time the archetype can be reused for the same purpose.

This ideal can be set up with or without the use of meditation and self-hypnosis. Some bad habits or personality traits rooted deeply in the person will require more time and effort to beat. For that intention self-hypnosis will certainly be of use. Once the person has gained useful habits and adequate level of mental discipline, self-hypnosis will be rarely used.

When using archetypes, the main idea is to find inspiration through imitation, not to limit one's self to the imitated model. Whatever the basis for the archetype is, one should not strive to become exactly like it, but to shape the model to suit their needs in the process of training. Archetypes are more of a tool that can be combined with other tools and left aside when they fulfill their purpose. A supreme goal or an ideal can also be considered an archetype of future self, one that you strive to realize or even surpass.

For the use of self-hypnosis to control emotions, archetypes such as a Jedi, or a Stoic can be used. The Jedi from The Star Wars are at least partially based on eastern philosophies, particularly on Buddhism. This is evident from their shared values of non-violence, search for wisdom, and keeping emotions in check.

One particularly useful part of Jedi philosophy are these three lines from the Jedi code[52]:

There is no emotion, there is peace./ There is no passion, there is serenity./ There is no chaos, there is harmony./

These three lines can be used for self-hypnosis during meditation as described before. As you repeat these lines in your mind try to understand what they imply. For this purpose it does not matter what they may mean in the context of films and games. It can be said that in that context, the Jedi code serves to give principles for the worldview in stoic sense. It gives the basics for the mentality which promotes action in accordance with reason instead of action influenced by emotions, very similar to stoic ideals.

The three lines of the code are fundamentally the same when examined in the context of meditation and single person. They can all be used to achieve inner peace and harmony from the usual chaos of passions and emotions. When using them during meditation try to connect their meaning with this idea.

There are two more lines of the Jedi code that are not useful for the aim of reducing intensity of emotions. One of them can be

---

52 Star Wars: Knights of the Old Republic, BioWare, LucasArts, 2003, video game

used as a part of archetype for self motivation towards acquisition of knowledge: *There is no ignorance, there is knowledge.* As it was mentioned before, ignorance is one of the causes of uncontrolled emotions. So this line also indirectly contributes to mental discipline. The last remaining line is more of speculative and religious nature, similar to the Buddhist worldview: *There is no death, there is the force.* In Buddhist philosophy there is no death or rebirth, but endless transformation of the complex of elements that constitute a person[53].

The archetype of a Stoic might not be as suitable as the Jedi archetype for reducing the intensity of emotions. General characteristics of Stoicism were discussed in the first chapter. Controlling emotions in the spirit of Stoicism means to use wisdom, knowledge, and understanding of the world and self in order to establish general indifference and inner peace, much like the Jedi depicted in the prequel movies. This is obvious in the writings like the mentioned *Meditations* by Marcus Aurelius.

Once a person understands the nature of events, their inevitability and the fact that once they happen, no matter what is done, events will not be undone; then the person will not react as

---

53 Veljačić, Č.,1983, *Filozofija istočnih naroda I,* Matica Hrvatska, Zagreb, p. 104; There are very few books by Veljačić translated in English, but the same data can be found in other books on Indian philosophy written by experts such as Otto Rosenberg, Surendranath Dasgupta and others.

emotionally as they originally would. There is no point in getting angry or sad about unchangeable facts because they will not change no matter how emotionally invested one gets. It is much better to simply move on and do what *can* be done, as it was mentioned before in the first chapter.

There is nothing in Stoicism as convenient as the Jedi code, but it can be invented based on stoic philosophy and the formulation of the Jedi code:

There is no emotion, there is indifference./ There is no passion, there is restraint./ There is no excess, there is temperance./ There is no suffering, there is endurance./

These lines of the newly formed "Stoic code" can be used in self hypnosis and in everyday life for controlling and reducing the intensity of emotions with the same effectiveness as the Jedi code. The archetype of a Stoic can also be called an archetype of the Sage. In ancient times philosophers aspired to become wise to that degree that they understand and know all the essential principles of life, in terms of ethics, natural philosophy, cosmology etc. Simply put, to obtain the highest possible knowledge in philosophy, like it was said before.

In Stoicism, as it was mentioned at the beginning, virtuous life is the life in accordance with natural law. The stoic sage would then be the person who understands this law fully and achieves perfect peace and tranquility through wisdom. It could be said that Socrates was described as such a sage in Platonic dialogues. Particularly in the dialogue *Phaedo*, where he meets his death sentence with absolute calmness.

To defend yourself from psychological abuse of verbal bullies passive indifference may not be enough. People who are too passive and agreeable, fundamentally incapable of violence and cruelty will inevitably become victims of people who *are* capable. Agreeable people will keep treating well those who are continuously rude to them, or keep harming them in any way, instead of demanding respect or cutting them out of their life. It is like the Stockholm syndrome, they justify their toxicity with bad life experiences they may have suffered. It all starts in childhood. As you grow up people will tell you that verbal bullies will stop if you ignore them, but it is not true. They will keep sapping your energy and make your life difficult until you start fighting back. Therefore it is important to cultivate your "dark side".

This does not mean you should act violently, get into physical fights for no reason, or inflict cruelty on others for its own sake. On the contrary, you should learn to develop your violent instincts, your hatred, and anger in a constructive way. Hot anger and hatred cause irrational behavior and lack of control. For example, if you are fed up with your boss you will impulsively yell, make a scene and quit.

On the other hand, cold hatred and anger can give you focus. They are controlled form of your violent instinct an as such they can be useful and positive. They are your pride, defiance, and self-defense. In this case if you are fed up with your boss, you will calmly and coldly quit or wait for the opportune moment to quit. You are in control of you actions and you do not feel helpless or victimized, but powerful instead. That way you will not make trouble for yourself when facing bullies, or let them disturb you at school or work.

Archetypes useful for this purpose are those that inspire power, fear, and strength: gods of war, magic, or death, the Sith from Star Wars, Nietzsche's Superman, and similar. Elements of this concept have already been expressed implicitly so brief explanation will suffice. The goal is to use any of these archetypes to inspire you to increase your physical and mental strength, in Nietzsche's terms, your power and will to power. Build up your defiance and will to fight back when being bullied. It is wrong to let the pressure move you towards self-destructive instincts, towards depression, feeling of helplessness, and suicidal thoughts. It is also wrong to develop tendencies to get revenge through physical violence and murder.

As it was mentioned before, the best "revenge" is to be happy and successful. So, use all your hatred, rage, and defiance as a fuel for self-improvement. Use it as an inspiration to become stronger, more knowledgeable and more capable in every sense. This is easier said than done. Negative emotions and urges must be shaped and directed in a positive way. Use the described emotion control techniques to gradually direct and harness the energy of your potentially negative instincts to make them into a useful and positive force. They must be controlled so that you can call upon them when you need them without impairing your judgment. Do not bother anyone, do not take or damage their property, and do not let anyone bother you. Do not pity the pathetic wretches that want to make your life miserable. Tell them a few well measured, harsh words to get them off your back. And if you are attacked physically do not hesitate to fight back if you can, or use dirty tactics to get an opening to escape. This mental state can be achieved through development of mental discipline as described in this book. As long as you are aware of the concept, it should not be too difficult to achieve it when you are mentally skilled enough.

Text like these mentioned lines of Jedi code can be much more effective than an invented text because people often find more inspiration within already established system. The system, all it contains and represents, leaves people who like it in "awe". This awe is precisely what gives so much power and influence to archetypes. This is what one should strive to exploit when using archetypes for the purpose of manipulating one's emotions and personality traits. Archetypes are present in everyday life through education, pop culture, video games etc. Everyone has them in their subconsciousness which makes them very useful and effective. To use them it is enough to choose one you like which complements the intention.

If used successfully in the described way self-hypnosis will cause drastic reduction in the intensity of the emotions of the user. If the technique is performed only once, emotions should restore to their previous state within few days. If it is performed once in few successive days, or once every few days, when the effects begin to weaken, their presence will be extended. The duration and the intensity of the effects may vary with every individual and the quality of their use of the described technique.

When the technique is used properly, it reduces emotions for over 90% under normal circumstances. Under the circumstances when one is usually under great emotional stress, the intensity of the emotions is reduced 20-40% at the beginning. However, it is difficult to keep them that way. With practice it is possible to improve the performance of the technique. The reader should keep in mind that there is no measuring unit for the intensity of emotions or even a way to measure it. This is just a rough estimate and everyone should determine the effectiveness of the technique themselves. Doing so will help them keep track of their progress and decide how, or if they want to improve it. It is generally very difficult to maintain emotions reduced over 90%, so one does not have to worry they will be less emotional than they wish. As for reducing emotions to zero, that is turning them completely off, it is difficult to say if it is possible in the true sense. Emotions arise from the subconscious processes which make most of human mind. Suffice to say that it is possible to control emotions to a degree that most people will find it satisfactory. It is only the matter of training. If you do not intend going to extremes, it may be useful to keep them reduced up to 25%. This should not impact your personal or professional life, but it will give you a more clear mind and boost your passive resistance to outside influences.

The purpose of the technique is to subject emotions to mind to a higher degree. It is not necessary to use it indefinitely but only as long as it takes for one to gain better understanding of emotions. To learn how it is to live without them, or at least with their intensity reduced. And the most importantly, to find mechanisms in your mind that allow better control of emotions. It is hard to truly understand the nature of emotions by observing them from the inside, while under their influence the entire life. It is like being drunk from birth and everyone around you is also constantly drunk. Suddenly, one day, you get sober and everyone around you is laughing for no reason and they sway while walking. Everyone would think that you are sad because you are not laughing like they do, and that you are walking funny because you can walk straight. They would even think that you are ill because you do not behave like they do.

This analogy demonstrates how different is the perception of reality with and without the average intensity of emotions. Thought process is usually highly influenced and clouded by emotions. Only by casting aside emotion, or by sobering up, will one be able to observe the nature of emotion objectively. This is important to learn, but what will you do afterwards is outside the scope of this book.

It is important to understand that using this technique, or any similar that one may find elsewhere or develop themselves, is by no means the same as what is called "suppressing emotions" in psychology. Suppressing emotions means to refuse to express them and suffer their effects in silence while pretending they are not there. This technique reduces the intensity, the potential of emotions, or prevents their formation completely. When the technique is undone after using it for a long period of time one will suffer no negative consequences, while suppressing emotions may cause psychological damage. In the case of the technique, there is control and discipline, while in the case of suppressing emotions there is lack of the two.

Absence of emotions or empathy will not excuse one for harmful actions they may want to justify by it. Ethics, morality and social laws are not based on emotions and empathy but on reason, justice, and social utility, or at least they should be. Absence of emotions or empathy is not the basis for crime either. Emotions like greed, anger, and hate combined with lack of rationality and self control are much more likely to cause one to commit crime than rational indifference. People who justify their crimes by saying "Satan made me do it", "I saw that in a video game", "It is because I read that in a book on mental discipline" are exploiting ignorance, fear, and irrationality of members of judicial systems. "Satan made me do it", the oldest trick in the book indeed. The only thing more ridiculous than that is the fact that people still fall for it. Similarly, some people justify their failures by blaming it on controversial books while others seek to defame these books to gain profit.

Effects of self-hypnosis based emotion control technique

The act of significantly reducing emotions after an entire life of using them to a high degree, may seem a drastic step. However, it is necessary for the mentioned purpose of subordination of the emotion to the mind. The effects are not permanent or irreversible. The technique does not take away the potential to feel emotions but drastically weakens it. Which means, in the usual mental state when nothing out of ordinary is happening, the subject will feel little to no emotions. In the stressful situation when the subject usually feels intense emotions, he will still feel them but with significantly lower intensity. This ability allows a higher rationality while making important decisions under stress. To gain complete control over emotions it is necessary to learn other techniques to which self-hypnosis is only one of the steps.

Drastically reducing one's own emotion potential will surely feel unusual. It might even be uncomfortable to some. This method is a bit forceful so one may feel inner emptiness along with the inner peace. Behavior of people is highly influenced by their emotions, so drastic reduction of emotions will result in change of their behavior too. To what degree, depends on their personality.

Dreams are also influenced by emotions so the change might

affect them too. If one has turned off emotions while awake, at the beginning they will not have that ability while sleeping. At this stage the person will normally feel emotions depending on the dream. If the technique is mastered and used for years it is retained even in dreams. At that stage the effects on the dreams that may had been present should disappear and it would take a really intense dream to cause an emotional response. Ordinary nightmares will be observed calmly like a movie. Only a really intimidating dream will cause fear.

Useful effects will surely outweigh those that the user may consider negative. Some of useful effects are increased concentration, calmness, faster mind, sharper senses, and more rational way of thinking. All these effects, both positive and negative, may vary from person to person depending on their lifestyle. The "negative" or "positive" view on the effects is a matter of personal preference. Even if one uses these techniques to sever emotional connection to people they know, there is no fundamental change. They will still know whom to respect, whom to avoid, to whom to trust or distrust, etc.

Fictional characters without emotions are invented by people who have emotions and cannot possibly imagine how would such a person behave. This is why there is such a wide variety of different characters of that type in works of fiction. The closest to truth could be considered the portrayal of Vulcans in the Star

Trek. But to reduce the way of thinking to pure logical reflection, as shown in the Star Trek, is to underestimate human intellect (or intellect of an intelligent being) and to highly overestimate the importance of emotions.

As mentioned before all the effects of self-hypnosis are reversible at early stage even if used for years. If the process is not repeated to prolong the duration, the effects will spontaneously and gradually disappear. How long will it take for effects to start weakening spontaneously depends on how long the technique was employed and how effectively. At later stages you can reach a state of high control of emotions and thoughts which should be irreversible. It will be mentioned later in this chapter. Reaching this state requires a lot of effort and dedication to training, so there is no reason to fear activating it by accident.

If one has lived with little or no emotion for a long time, the process of restoring emotions might be interesting and equally unusual as reducing the emotions at the beginning. Since the individual is used to reduced emotions, their original intensity might feel strong. When one is habituated to the original state of emotions, they will feel like they originally did. Mental abilities gained in the process will remain intact. Those abilities are the goal of this entire procedure, and simply put, a higher level of mental discipline. Mental discipline includes increased mental abilities (concentration, willpower, rationality, awareness, self control), better understanding of emotions themselves, and a higher level of control over emotions.

When you get used to reduced intensity or potential of emotions things essentially do not change much. It just takes a stronger stimuli to cause an emotional reaction. When it comes to your attitude to other people, it will not change, only the scale is a bit different. For example, if your normal emotional output is 10, and your attitude towards person A is 6 and person B is 4. If you reduce the maximum intensity of emotions to 8, the attitude towards A will reduce to 5, and towards B to 3. So in essence everything is the same, but you are less sensitive to outside influences. Emotions do not have as strong influence on your thought process, which is the main advantage and the goal of maintaining this state. How far will you go with reducing your emotions is a matter of personal preference. However, it is important to take into consideration that this ability at this level also has a drawback, unlike early stages. If you do a job that relies on expression of emotions like art, or line of work that requires empathy or compassion, it may have a negative influence on your performance.

It is possible to initiate the process of restoring emotions willingly by using self-hypnosis again to negate its previous effects. While meditating induce a trance and observe the idea of emotions. Try to induce some of the basic ones, such as happiness, love, anger, etc. Use a line like emotions on, emotions are restored, or something similar. Reinforce the intention by inducing a feeling of joy and good will. Remember the social interactions with your friends and family and try to restore your original emotional reactions. This should help initiate restoring your emotional potential to its original state.

As before, an archetype can be used in this process too. Something like an archetype of a good natured neighbor would be of use. Characteristics of such an archetype can be philanthropy, good will, compassion, mild manners etc. This can be a good framework for restoration of normal emotional state.

Another method is to deliberately induce emotions using willpower and visualizations. This is done in a similar manner as auto-suggestion, but instead of focusing on a command one is focused on a concept of an emotion they are trying to induce. Using this method to increase the intensity of a spontaneous emotional reaction in everyday life will improve its effectiveness. Gradually your habit of emotional reactions will restore and emotions will form naturally as they originally did.

People who know the user of these and similar techniques of emotion control will surely notice the change in user's behavior.

Others who do not know them, will notice the general unusual behavior. To avoid drawing unnecessary attention, one can emulate the usual emotional reactions and facial expressions. If emotions are practically non existent, there is no basis for easy emulation. In that case one would have to mimic usual behavior by memory and reflex that remained from before the technique was applied. Other, easier method, is to allow formation of weak emotions that serve as basis for emulating usual responses. These weak emotions are mostly not strong enough to trigger the usual behavior (smiling, laughing, frowning, changing voice intonation, choosing words carefully, etc.) so it is necessary to reestablish the habit of performing such actions. The habit will disappear only if the person spends a lot of time alone. Social people will have much stronger habits of this type. In addition, some people are generally fake in their social interactions. In their case, no one will notice the difference.

How exactly will one hide their mental state or will they hide it at all, depends on personal preference. One may choose to be completely blunt about expressing their opinion, disregarding the oversensitive sentiment of the average people. They can speak in a mild manner or just say what others expect them to say. It is possible to remain completely expressionless, react only if they feel like it or just emulate emotions like others would expect.

Everyone is free to shape their personality as they see fit, according to their preferences and principles. It would be wise, however, to keep in mind that average people are often fearful and irrational. If they feel intimidated by someone, they may cause them unjustified social problems. Whoever does not fit into the mold of normality will often be considered strange at best, and evil or dangerous at worst, and as such will be feared and discriminated against. For that matter it would be the best to keep the ability to manipulate your emotions a secret, even from friends and family who may react negatively. In fact, they do not need to know in the first place.

This description is just a rough estimate of the possible and most probable effects of the mentioned technique. It would do no good to go in any more details. Everyone will be able to identify the effects by experience and introspection. It should not take long to become proficient in this particular method itself, considering only its effective use, but to gain the basis of the aimed mental discipline and knowledge may take 3-6 months of maintaining the reduced potential of emotions. How long exactly, as with all mental exercises, depends on the individual in question.

Inducing the trance state without meditation

The purpose of the previous exercise was to learn how to induce a trance state by meditation and to use self-hypnosis to gain higher level of mental discipline, primarily the control of emotions. The next step is to learn how to induce a state of trance without meditation which extends the usage of mental skills acquired by meditation and develops them further.

Inducing a trance without meditation is very similar to the process of inducing it by using meditation. The only difference is that it is done faster, and with the possibility of moving by making use of the abilities developed by meditation. To induce a trance in general, it is enough to change the usual active and analytical mental state into a more passive and focused one by concentrating on a single action or idea. One can learn how to do this without difficulty with a little practice if they have grasped the basics of meditation mentioned before.

The purpose of this skill is to employ a higher degree of mental discipline in everyday life. More specifically, it allows direct control of one's own mental state, and thus control of emotions and instincts. This paves a way for a large area of possibilities for practical use of mental discipline which will be described later in the book.

Here are some guidelines how to learn to induce a trance without meditating:

1. While sitting or standing, relax and focus just on your breathing. Maintain the focus for few seconds and passively observe your mental state. It should start to change towards a trance within 30 seconds. Closing your eyes for a few seconds may help at the beginning. Later it will not be necessary. This simple exercise will serve well to notice the change between the two mental states out of meditation, much like it had been learned during the meditation.

2. Relax, clear your mind, and keep it clear for a few seconds while observing your mental state as in the previous tip. Closing your eyes briefly may help in this case too. Relaxed intention to change one's mental state can help in any case, but forcing the change may have the opposite effect.

3. Focusing on repetitive movement also induces the trance. If you are walking, sweeping, dancing, practicing one same martial arts move, etc. and you focus on the required body movement and maintaining proper breathing while blocking out all other thoughts will cause similar effects as in previous tips.

All these tips have in common the act of focusing on a single action, or an idea. Because of that it can be called a form of meditation, but it is more of a technique to focus your mind. Meditation in literal sense is concentrated and lengthy exercise. When meditating, one takes time to relax and prepare before performing the exercise that spontaneously causes the trance. When someone wishes to induce a trance without meditation as described in this book, the preparation is skipped and the experience and willpower previously gained from meditation is used to induce a trance at will. This will is precisely what can make a difference between successful and failed attempt. To succeed it is enough to simply *will* to induce a trance while focusing on a single object of thought (visualization, act of breathing) or maintain vacancy of mind for a short period of time. As always, it might be hard to succeed at the beginning but with practice and persistence it should not take long to grasp the basics. After a while of using the skill it becomes as easy as breathing to induce a trance at will.

Trance induced as described here is milder in comparison to the trance induced by meditation. The reason for that is, obviously, because of the longer preparation and generally more suitable circumstances for the induction of a deeper trance. The depth of the induced trance depends on the skill and intention of the user. The higher the focus and the duration of meditation the deeper the trance. Concerning the meditative practice in general, this is not something out of ordinary. When you meditate you do not exactly aim to induce a trance, but you inevitably reach that state as a matter of course. The deeper the meditation the more you are "separated" from the outside world, which is nothing else than a trance. You should strive to reach as deep meditation as possible in every session because is the most beneficial for your training.

Techniques mentioned thus far are some of the simplest and safest for inducing a trance. There are a lot of other techniques that require ingestion of chemicals like alcohol or various hallucinogens. Other techniques require tiring the body in some way like with sleep deprivation, sensory deprivation, fasting, flagellation, dancing and drumming till exhaustion, etc. Similar techniques are mostly used in religious and magic rituals. These more demanding methods, if done without caution, may cause more harm than good. In addition they can not be used as frequently as the basic techniques described in this book. They may serve their purpose better than other methods, but for the purpose of self-improvement simple basic techniques are more suitable. At the end it all comes down to personal goals and preferences.

After a while of using trances, when the user is used to them, they will also become a normal mental state. Normal mental state can be called any state that the user is comfortable with, a state induced and/or maintained on purpose. Really abnormal states are only those that arise against the will, such as panic, anxiety, lack of focus, mind overwhelmed with emotions, etc.

Practical applications of self-hypnosis

The benefit of inducing a trance at will is in the possibility to use self-hypnosis whenever it is needed. Without that ability one is able to maintain the intensity of emotions or imprint other auto-suggestions into subconsciousness only when they have enough time for meditation, which is not the case at all times. With practice and experience one is able to use auto-suggestion effectively even without inducing a trance.

To maintain the desired intensity of emotions, one can use the same auto-suggestion that they used during the meditation after inducing a trance as described previously. That method is less effective because of the milder trance and lower degree of focus, but it can prolong the effects of meditation. If used frequently, the effects can be prolonged from days of duration to weeks or months. Effectiveness of the skill will increase with practice.

Frequent repetition of associating an intention or an idea with an action will strengthen that connection and increase the quality of the desired effect. For example if one wants to reduce their emotions (intention or idea), they use an auto-suggestion in a chosen way (action), and it causes the effect of reducing the emotions. That same procedure if repeated frequently becomes like a program in subconsciousness that will always run the same if it is triggered by the mind. If one restores their emotions after a long time of using the same technique to reduce their potential, they can reduce it again instantly if they use the same mental trigger with intention. They can think about existence of the "program" and the "trigger" and what it does, but it will not activate without intention to do so. One has to invest certain mental effort and willpower to literally will it to be. If one does not put harmful commands into their subconsciousness, there is no danger of using such techniques.

It is possible to use similar methods to negate not only emotions in general, but particular undesirable emotions, instincts, and urges. Using these methods for extended period of time will make them more effective simply because one gains more skill, higher willpower, and mental discipline in general, but it does not reach the same level of a single precise intention. Such singular intentions are suitable for specific tasks that are of use for longer period of time (i.e. emotion control, changing habits), while general mental discipline extends to general use whenever it is required. The goal of the practice described here is in gaining general mental discipline which can be useful in every aspect of life.

In the state of reduced output of emotions, instincts and urges are also weaker so it is easier to control them. Thus, that state is an excellent environment for the initial changing of habits. As mentioned in the first chapter, one may break a bad habit by repeatedly not doing the habitual action. If one has the habit of smoking they wish to break, in this environment when the impulse to smoke is significantly reduced it is easier to quit smoking. Another useful method for such purposes is using auto-suggestion to remove the desire. The next method is to use self-hypnosis to reinforce your will not to smoke and create disgust for cigarettes. As Bardon[54] says, commands used for auto-suggestion or self-hypnosis should be in present imperative form: I do not smoke, I do not like smoking, smoking makes me sick.

Based on this example one can easily think of a way to break other bad habits. To form a new useful habit, one can simply repeat the action in regular time intervals. To make it easier to uphold, one can reinforce the will to do so by self-hypnosis or auto-suggestions. Philosophical view and goals in life can greatly

54 Bardon, F., 2018, *Initiation Into Hermetics*, Merkur Publishing, USA, p. 82

help in choosing how to form one's own personality, including the choice of good habits and finding the reason and motivation to uphold them. For this purpose the use of philosophy is explained in the first chapter.

The use of auto-suggestion is not only limited to influencing one's own emotions, instincts, and urges, but it can be used for wide variety of tasks. In addition, it is not limited only to verbal commands, existing words, or a single language. Intention or idea can be bound to hand gestures, body postures, newly invented words, mental images, spoken words, sounds, etc. That which makes any of these, or similar means effective is repetition. Someone may find certain methods more inspiring, to be more specific, methods they consider "cool" are more effective, as it was mentioned with archetypes. Using Latin, ancient Greek, other foreign language, made up words and phrases, exotic hand gestures like ninjas in pop culture, or meditation mudras etc. can be initially more effective for any purpose if they are mentally stimulating for the user. If the user is completely indifferent, repetition of the intention, action, and the desired effect is that which makes it equally effective in the end. It is advisable to keep these methods secret to avoid attracting unnecessary attention, especially in the case of means perceivable by others, such as hand gestures or sounds.

It is possible to use a self-hypnosis command to wake up at certain time. Combining a command with intention and an idea of a specific time will make this happen. If the user went to sleep too late and did not have enough time to rest, the command will not work because it is necessary for body to rest and that necessity is of higher priority.

Another similar use is to be reminded of an obligation or something similar at a specific time. It is done the same way as the previous example. General success of these uses of self-hypnosis depend on the skill of the user. It is not necessary to practice these particular skills to use them effectively, it is enough to be good at using self-hypnosis in general.

Those interested in exploring the dream state can use self-hypnosis before falling asleep to remember more of the contents of their dreams and make them more coherent. This can be of great use for those who want to keep record of their dreams. Remembering the dreams can also be considered a first step for inducing lucid dreaming. A self-hypnosis command is one of the methods employed for that purpose too. Since dream state is quite different from the awake state, it may be more difficult to have success at that field. It does respond to general skill in self-hypnosis, but it may require additional practice to become proficient.

If one has trouble falling asleep, they can use regular meditation techniques to relax and bring the mind closer to the dream state. Meditation is in between the active and dreaming state of mind. Once the person is relaxed, they can use a self-hypnosis command to "persuade" themselves into falling asleep sooner, or to make themselves more relaxed. To succeed in the intent, all they have to do is be careful not to return their mind into the active state after self-hypnosis is employed, but maintain relaxed focus on random thoughts without thinking hard about anything, which will cause them to fall asleep. This may also help with with real insomnia, but it is hard to tell to what degree without testing it. If the insomnia is not caused by anything psychological, these techniques may only alleviate the problem, not solve it. Meditation in general may be of help there too, but to what degree depends on the individual case.

Practitioners of martial arts or sports can realize a large part of their potential if they develop mental discipline. Improved concentration and introspection allows better analysis of the training progress. It is possible to monitor how fast you get tired, and how your body and muscles move while performing exercises. With that ability one is able to learn by experience much more about their strengths and weaknesses than they would otherwise. More precisely, to polish their techniques far more effectively, to understand how a technique is used properly, correct their body stances, etc. True, these skills can certainly be learned through experience without mental training. But with mental training and philosophic approach the learning process is faster and more precise. In other words, you learn at earlier stages of study/training what you would otherwise learn much later.

Another great benefit is self control and calmness in crisis. In sports or martial arts, if your mind is clouded by emotions, it gets hard to time reactions, assess the opponent, and plan ahead. Angry attacks are predictable and they waste energy. Disciplined individual is hard to provoke, and will assess themselves and their abilities rationally, as well as the abilities of the opponent. Panicking, rushing, overestimating or underestimating the abilities of one's self, or the opponent may be dangerous, especially in a real self defense scenario. This can also translate to everyday life as rational behavior in dangerous situations where ordinary people panic and behave erratically.

Practitioners of martial arts or sports will easily discover the benefits of developed mental discipline themselves. Mastering only physical part of such an activity is only a half of mastery, because one can only realize their entire potential if they develop both the mind and the body. For those who are not interested in martial arts or sports, related examples can give ideas for other applications of described skills. If nothing else, these examples serve to show the flexibility of mental discipline.

During the meditation, in the state of vacant mind, one may notice that along with thoughts, emotions also disappear. Emotions are formed by processing the data of thoughts. If there is no thought, there is no emotion either. If one is thinking about something unpleasant it will cause formation of negative emotions. If they think about something positive it will create positive emotions. The goal is to learn to see things for what they are, to observe them objectively with or without emotion as one sees fit.

Emotions formed from thoughts are an important part of the complete spectrum of human emotions, but it is also important to keep in mind that emotions also form from the subconsciousness. These emotions can be felt in the back of your mind, but with experience and discipline the influence of these emotions can be reduced and resisted.

People often say that you cannot choose who or what you love, and like phrases, as an excuse for poor choices regarding their love interest and irrational infatuation. This lack of control is obviously false. That which causes love, besides the base instinct of sexual attraction, is thinking positively about the person or anything else one may love. If you are thinking about positive aspects of something or someone, you will spontaneously feel positive emotions like love, liking, attraction, etc. Conversely for the opposite. If you willingly prevent the formation of such emotions, you may objectively observe the object of thought. Appreciate it, respect it, admire it, or the opposite, without developing the state of love or hate in any intensity. If you willingly think about positive or negative traits of an object of thought, while allowing the formation of the corresponding emotions, you will allow yourself to develop the state of love or hate. Simply put, if you control your thoughts you also control emotions. Regardless of the subconsciousness, thoughts strongly guide the way emotions are formed.

By using this principle it is possible to fall in love, hate, or neither at will. It is ill advised to accommodate other people by meeting their expectations by creating emotions they may expect of you, or what only appears they expect. Such "artificially" formed emotions, even though they may seem fake, are equally real as those formed spontaneously, and as such will cause the same emotional or mental harm if directed at undeserving people.

Some people will use their sex appeal or charisma to induce certain emotions in others with intention of exploiting them in any way they want. They use passive aggressiveness, emotional blackmail, impose guilt, play a victim, act helpless, seductive, friendly, loving, etc. to entice people to do them favors without asking directly, thus avoiding responsibility of returning the favor. Keeping emotions in check to rationally estimate the circumstances and possible intentions of people, allows one to defend against such psychic vampires.

Based on the fact that processing thought data causes formation of emotion, maintaining the vacant mind for few seconds is the easiest way to get rid of unwanted emotions in any given situation. If one is panicking, as an example of an extreme case, clearing the mind will help them regain composure to act rationally.

Another, similar way to prevent formation of an unwanted emotion is to remove the object of thought that caused it to form. This happens spontaneously while someone gets engrossed in an activity, playing a computer game for example, and they do not notice they are hungry until it becomes intense enough. One can induce this mental state at will by removing, in this case, the idea of wanting to eat or idea of specific food that came to their mind. Removing the cause of the problem, removes the problem itself. With practice you can easily remove simple yet persistent irritants from your consciousness.

You can learn how to do this during meditation. It is done the same way as blocking thoughts unrelated to the meditation exercise. Essentially, whenever an undesirable emotion or outside stimuli appears simply empty your mind for a second and move your attention to something more important. By removing the cause of the undesired emotion, emotion itself ceases to exist. By focusing on something useful or more interesting afterwards, you reduce the chances the irritation will influence you. That is the way to apply this skill in everyday life. There are other techniques that extend the use of meditation based emotion control which will be described in the next chapter.

Emotions, impulses, and instincts are often activated by association with specific "triggers" in the environment. For example if someone sees or smells food they will start feeling hungry, often even in case they do not really need to eat. Sexual attraction is often triggered when someone sees a person they consider attractive in that sense. If one dwells on, or immerses themselves in instincts aroused in such a way, the cause and effect will become a habit. Sometimes such habits may become distracting. For example, someone may find it difficult to work in the presence of the opposite sex. Someone may be unable to resist the smell of food, eat too often, and become obese. If someone finds emotional comfort in eating or getting drunk, it can cause addiction. There are many possible problems that can be created by forming such harmful habits.

To make it easier to break habits, along with previously mentioned methods, it is possible to mentally disassociate the cause and the instinct. A simple way to do this is to think of the cause, for example food, feel its effect, in this case hunger, and simply will the connection between the two to disappear. If this is too hard to do, another way is to remove the cause as previously described. If you keep removing the cause it will gradually break the habit. If the cause and effect are disassociated there will be no more distractions and the one will become immune to the specific environmental influence.

The end goal is to form a mentality where you do everything at its own time. For example if you are professionally working with people as a waiter, shop employee, photographer, or other similar work you should be unaffected by possible sexual advances of your customers. Even if you engage in trivial conversations as part of the job, the mental discipline should prevent you from taking it any further than professional. When in a non professional setting you will not have such inhibitions. Another example would be, if you are going home hungry from work, you should be unaffected by the smell of food if you intend eating at home.

These examples may seem banal, but they serve well to explain how mental discipline can be used. The focus on the purpose of the activity you are doing is what prevents you from straying from our plans, especially if the focus is reinforced by principles. In what circumstances and to what degree will you be "focused", how will you implement it on habitual actions and everyday life is matter of personal preference and principle.

Using these principles of making or removing emotions, impulses, and instincts by controlling one's own thoughts, one can shape their entire personality at will. Breaking a bad habit, forming a new and useful one, changing the way of speaking in general, way of thinking, principles, beliefs, interests, etc. and in the end you are a completely different person. One may ask "what if these methods are used for a long time? What if you forget who you really are?" There is no *true* or *false self,* there is only one *self*. There is no need to search hard for that original *"I"*. The feeling or conception of self never changes, even though entire personality may change. People change constantly during their life, some only slightly, others significantly. In that case one may say that they are a different person, and it may be considered true from a certain point of view, but the new personality is still a property, a characteristic, an attribute of the same individual.

It is also important to take into consideration that, as Nietzsche once said "The will to overcome an emotion, is ultimately only the will of another, or of several other emotions."[55] Overcoming

---

55 Nietzsche, F., 2013, *Al di là del bene e del male,* Adelphi, Milano, chap. 4, 117.

all of your instincts and submitting them to reason may be hard or even impossible, but every one you manage to overcome will reduce the limits on the freedom of will. The reader will easily decide themselves how useful are the described techniques on this matter.

The use of advanced meditation techniques

Once the basic meditation techniques have been practiced long enough for developing sufficient concentration and skill, it is advisable to move on to more complex techniques. Sufficient concentration and skill means that the practitioner:

1. is able to notice the effects of meditation
2. is able to induce a trance at will
3. is able to maintain the focus on the exercise for 3-5 minutes without their thoughts wandering off
4. will not easily fall asleep during meditation
5. can maintain proper posture and breathing with little or no effort

Without a solid foundation it is hard to perform advanced meditation exercises effectively. To be able to perform an advanced meditation exercise for 10 minutes, or even a few minutes without an error may take months to achieve. Without a strict exercise it takes too much time for significant improvement. The effort and persistence will be rewarded with higher degree of mental discipline. To be more specific, a person who practices meditation properly for years will gradually surpass some of the social concepts and some of their own core beliefs. It takes time to fully and truly discard conditioning and programming imposed by the society on an individual. Such concepts are surpassed once the individual sees that such concepts are empty and void of meaning for their life. These concepts to be surpassed may be nationality, religion, trivial friendship, wealth, fitting in with others, political power, fame, romantic relationships, hedonistic goals, to name just a few. Which concept, and how will one see it afterwards, depends on what type of person they are.

By "surpassing" it is not implied anything in religious sense, like realizing the "sin" of such concepts, but to see them in completely new light. The way that one thinks it is true, not the way they were taught to think by authority figures or the society in general. This perspective is achieved by combining rational and critical philosophical thinking with development of mind and insight through meditation.

Religious or non religious groups often give their members preformed system of philosophy to reflect upon. Even though it may contain some, or even a great deal of wisdom, in most cases it leads to dogmatism and indoctrination. What could be considered a better alternative is, as mentioned before, to develop one's own philosophy to follow and develop during the life, while evading dogmatism and self-deception.

One specific concept of importance that can be surpassed, which the reader probably already noticed, are emotions. Effects of self-hypnosis alone used to limit their potential are reversible, but general effort put into submitting emotions to mind combined with frequent meditation will cause one to surpass emotions themselves in a sense, but not in the true sense of the word. This stage is irreversible. The entire process of controlling your emotional intensity with the use of meditation and self-hypnosis is more dynamic than static. You may rest between periods of meditation, but you will more likely use some out-of-meditation techniques to support the effects of meditation. As you use these methods you develop the skill of controlling emotions and thoughts. Once you learn it, you cannot unlearn it. Even if you do not actively use it, it is still present in you mind and you can rely on it instantly if needed. In addition, a part of your discipline remains as a reflex. In that state emotions and thoughts are highly subordinated to the mind, or the will. It is irreversible because once the nature of emotions is seen, it can no longer be unseen.

Your invested effort and developed ability cannot be undone. This stage of mental development is much more flexible and suitable for general use. It surpasses the use of self-hypnosis for purpose of manipulating emotions. Potential of emotions is highly reduced like with the use of self-hypnosis, but in this case it is no longer forced. Emotions form naturally with the permission of the user, though their intensity is considerably weaker than originally. At that stage a person can enjoy all things in life naturally, but the intellectual part of joy is significantly more pronounced than the usual instinctive. One specific skill developed in this stage is to directly influence one's emotions with their mind. To nullify them or to transform them at will. This skill will be explained in the next chapter because it is not based on meditation or self-hypnosis.

One needs not fear activating that state in the early stages of developing mental discipline because at that point everything is reversible and it is possible to give up the training if the one does not like its effects. It is also possible to choose a different course which does not lead to that particular skill. If one has kept on going for years using the described techniques of this manual, they will most likely welcome that stage of development. That stage is where this manual leads, but not necessarily. It is still not mastery of mental discipline because it is still not complete immunity to outside influences, it does not provide full control over emotions and thoughts. It certainly is a great leap in progress from the beginning, but not the full realization of the personal potential. The "system" that is primarily highlighted in this book emphases reason and logic over emotion and compassion. There are other systems that emphasize the opposite. The reader is, as always, free to choose how will they use the described skills and how will they develop themselves.

An important thing to consider regarding the surpassing of certain concepts, or the will to cast them aside, is that it has to be effortless. If one wishes to cast aside, for example, romantic relationships, and they have to mentally and emotionally struggle to succeed, it means it is too early for them to do so. Such struggles can only lead to desperation and damage mental health. If one is able to abstain from romantic relationships, or any other similar concept or activity without regrets and mental struggle, it is possible to say that they have successfully cast it aside.

Regarding the difference between casting aside and surpassing, "to surpass" is defined here as a spontaneous rejection of an idea, a social concept, or an activity by realizing its uselessness and insignificance for the life of an individual in question. In this case a person naturally becomes indifferent towards a concept or idea and is not interested in practicing it. "To cast aside" is the act of deliberate long term rejection of an idea, a social concept, or an activity without any regrets or mental struggle required to succeed in the intention to do so.

In this case a person deliberately becomes indifferent towards a concept or an idea. Both of these concepts are a result of mental training. The reasons to cast aside or to surpass something can be numerous. They depend on personal goals, views, and preferences. One of the best reasons can be to become free of socially or self imposed slavery which certain concepts and activities bring. The term "surpass" as defined in this book is only valid in this context, not in general sense of the word.

Asceticism

The concept of asceticism was mentioned multiple times in the book but it was not explained. In religious practice asceticism can take many forms: fasting, living in poverty, abstinence from comfort and physical pleasures, sleep deprivation, flagellation, living simple and minimalist lifestyle, etc. It is especially characterized by strictness, seriousness, and dedication. It could thus be said that professional athletes and lifelong practitioners of crafts, martial arts, science, art, literature, etc. are ascetic in a sense.

The purpose of asceticism depends on the respective religion of practice. It is mostly used in eastern religions to shift attention from the physical towards the spiritual in search of enlightenment. In Abrahamic religions it is mostly used for self-punishment and purification from sin. For example, in the middle ages, Christians used asceticism to get closer to the simple life of Jesus. On the other hand, they used self torture to get closer to the torment of Christ and martyred saints.

Generally speaking, for asceticism to be useful it must be done seriously as a form of training with self-improvement in mind. This correlates with the original meaning of the word which, among other things, referred to rigorous self-discipline and training[56]. If it is done to conform with religion without thinking about it and without understanding it leads nowhere. For example, fasting in modern Catholicism is mostly done as a routine prescribed by the religion with no deeper meaning.

Practices like flagellation and the goal of self-punishment are useless at best, and self-destructive at worst. You cannot do much training with broken body and mind. Such masochism is more an example of fanaticism and mental illness than dedication to the absolute. On the other hand, moderate abstinence from comfort and physical pleasures can be useful if done properly.

Proper use of asceticism depends on personal ability and

---

[56] https://www.etymonline.com/word/ascetic?ref=etymonline_crossreference (Jan/30/2018)

preference. For example, one cannot use rigorous physical training for this purpose if they are not physically fit enough. In that case they would have to develop basic level of fitness as a preparation for such training, or choose a different form of asceticism. Serious and regular physical exercise can be beneficial for everyone which makes it a very useful element of ascetic practice. Another element which can be combined with physical exercise is meditation, as mentioned before. That which makes asceticism different from regular exercise is the effort put in it and the sense of strain and discipline that arises from the exercise. Occasional light or medium exercises cannot be considered ascetic, but frequent, strenuous, and serious exercise can certainly be considered ascetic.

Another mentioned useful element of asceticism is abstinence. This does not have to be permanent or taken to any extreme as it is done in religion, however some elements can be useful for long term practice. Minimalism and moderation can be a form of long term asceticism depending on their intensity. If one strives for buying only absolutely necessary things, they will not only free up space in their home, but also save money. If your house/apartment happens to be on the smaller side, if you furnish it only with necessities it will not feel too small. Minimalist element does not have to be taken to the extreme of having only a pair of shoes and a pair of pants, but it is wasteful and unnecessary to buy a full closet of clothes that will rarely be used, if ever.

Moderation in food, drink, sex, and entertainment will save time, money, effort, and health. In addition it will maximize their pleasure. For example, when people eat too much food they love, gradually they get desensitized and they need more and more to feel satisfied. Thus they get overweight and spend too much money on food. It is similar with other mentioned pleasures: excess alcohol causes health risks and discomfort of nausea and hangover; promiscuity wastes money and time, in addition to the risk of STI-s, unwanted marriage and children, false sexual abuse charges etc.

Avoiding certain specially tasty but unhealthy food and drink may be useful to start healthier eating habits, but other than that it will not do much more than reinforcing the feeling of self discipline and spartan lifestyle. Avoiding sex and masturbation on the other hand, my be useful to channel your time and energy into other more productive activities. For example, time may be better spent working, doing mental and physical training, studying, reading, etc.

A short term form of abstinence can be solitude, which is abstinence from social interactions. As it was mentioned before, solitude is very useful for introspection and mental training because it isolates a person from outside influences and distractions. Isolation can be considered ascetic because it is mentally hard to endure for most people. In addition, the mental state it causes can be both pleasant and tiring in a unique way. It cannot be done long term in the most cases because it is necessary to work for living and to buy things like groceries. Shopping and working requires social interactions. Only someone who grows their own food can live in longterm isolation. However, modern technology allows the practice of "urban hermitage" without the need to grow food yourself. You can order groceries on-line without having to interact with the people who provide the service. If you work at home you can extend the hermitage practically indefinitely. Other solitary people, if they must interact with coworkers and clients during work hours, can spend their vacation in isolation.

To put all said about asceticism into practice, the most suitable ascetic elements can be combined and practiced for a period of time, maybe a week or more if your schedule allows it. For example, a combination of solitude, physical exercises, reading, and meditation can be very useful. As mentioned before, reducing social interactions to a minimum allows a quality introspection and meditative state of mind. Meditation, in addition to mental training, changes the general mental state. Physical exercise when combined with meditation, as it was said on movement meditation, extends the use of stationary meditation and prolongs its effects. In addition, physical exertion reinforces the sense of asceticism. When all these three, or more similar practices are combined, they produce a unique mental state. When extended long enough they will result in a form of catharsis that clears your mind from stress, trivial worries, and useless information. It may also result in a significant improvement of mental discipline. It is important to keep in mind that results of this training are subjective as all mental training is. As such they vary from person to person depending on their preferences, predisposition, level of skill, and the intensity of the training.

In order to succeed in this practice, it is important to be as focused as possible for its entire duration. You must let yourself be immersed in the training. This will be possible only if the required mentality is developed during the general training of mental discipline. For that reason such exercises may be suitable only for practitioners who mastered the basics of meditation, and can do more advanced meditation techniques like the breathing exercise, or visualization of geometric shapes. Without the basics it would be hard to maintain the required mental state and the solitude would be too much of a burden. The entire training would be more of a self-torture than a strengthening experience. People who are not yet at the stage of training where they can do this type of exercise will benefit from moderate asceticism as previously described.

In terms of mental discipline, the primary goal of this book is passive indifference as opposed to active effort to be indifferent. When built up through training it is already prepared when you face a negative stimuli. You can effortlessly resist it without doing anything more. Active techniques like rationalization, self-hypnosis, auto-suggestion, and willpower based emotion control are useful in a situation when your passive indifference is not strong enough. In that case you have to invest certain effort to make yourself indifferent. This effort further builds up your passive indifference through mentioned techniques and regular meditation. It creates thought patterns and habits that reduce your emotional sensitivity. In other words, as you practice over time you simply care less and less about things that are irrelevant to you. What is relevant or not depends on your philosophic views. So in summary, the goal is to develop a passive indifference so strong that you need to rely on active techniques very rarely, if ever. As it was mentioned, emotional insensitivity has its drawbacks so it is the matter of personal preference to what degree will you develop it. It ranges from the point where it is nonexistent to the point where you care about nothing and no one but yourself and your own benefit.

Summary

In this chapter mental discipline is finally described as intended in this book. Through practice of meditation we learn how to focus our thoughts, which also makes emotions easier to control. For successful meditation it is important to breathe naturally and deeply from the diaphragm. Relax mentally and physically, do not be anxious about results. Meditation should be effortless, so avoid straining your mind. Do not think about what will you do later, or about your troubles. Immerse yourself in the exercise instead.

Regular meditation makes you calmer and more focused in general and increases your passive indifference mentioned in the first chapter. If the negative outside stimuli is too strong for passive indifference, clear your mind and focus on your breathing for a few seconds. It will remove the irritation from your mind and reset your thoughts and emotions. This procedure also induces a meditative mental state and prolongs the effects of previous meditative exercises.

The upgraded version of auto-suggestion is self-hypnosis. It is the second active skill used to control your emotions. To use that skill, induce a trance by going into deep meditation. Then use an auto-suggestion like you normally would. The deeper meditative state will cause the auto-suggestion to have significantly stronger and longer lasting effect. Self-hypnosis can be used to break or establish habits as necessary. It can also be used to cause the state of weakened emotions which contributes to passive indifference and mental discipline in general.

The effects of meditation and self-hypnosis weaken over time. To prolong them empty your mind and focus on breathing for a few seconds. Keep this state for a short while and use your experience to induce a mild trance. This state allows you to use auto-suggestion on the move, reducing your dependency on stationary meditation.

Long term effort in controlling emotions and thoughts increases your overall passive indifference, and thus your mental discipline. Techniques you learn grow more effective and their use becomes a habit. With time it becomes effortless to change your inner state at will. Emotions and thoughts become highly subordinated to willpower. This is the irreversible stage of mental training. At this stage you spontaneously reject certain concepts, habits, or patterns of behavior. You can also deliberately reject them at will. Deliberate rejection must be effortless, otherwise it causes psychological harm.

Chapter 3:
Energy manipulation

Introduction

In this chapter an "occult" skill called energy manipulation will be explained. In theory, it allows the user to manipulate the Subtle Energy in and out of their body. For the purpose of this book, it is completely irrelevant if the ability is real, or just illusion caused by bio feedback. The practice can be observed as a form of meditation, and its application can be used to develop the ability to control your emotions by willpower alone. This skill can be acquired by previously mentioned practices, but the exercises in this chapter are more specific and deliberate for that purpose.

By using this skill it is possible to greatly increase the control over emotions and instincts. It allows one to dissolve them at will, which will be explained later in the book. Mental discipline acquired by meditation exercises described in the previous chapter will make learning techniques described here easier. Energy manipulation is primarily a mental skill. Learning to use it and developing it further also develops mental discipline.

The term occult is derived from Latin word *occultus* which means hidden[57]. This is the original meaning of the term. It is also defined in the dictionaries as something that deals with hidden

---

57 Online Etymology Dictionary: http://etymonline.com/index.php?allowed_in_frame=0&search=occult (May/12/2017)

forces of nature. That can not be correct because every occult system defines the laws according to which occult abilities behave. This definition is now more present in everyday conversation. It could be said that "occult" is the same as "esoteric"[58], which is derived from ancient Greek word *esōterikós* which means on the inside or intimate. In some ancient Greek schools of philosophy there were esoteric teachings, reserved only for the closed circle of its students, and exoteric teachings which were considered suitable for general public. That meaning seems more suitable, therefore occult does not imply hidden forces of nature but teachings reserved only for a closed circle of people, hidden from everyone else. Such teachings were indeed kept secret for centuries and they started spreading to a wider public during the late Medieval period and the Renaissance. One of the main reasons for secrecy could be the prosecution and execution of "heretics" by the Church. Another important reason may have been to prevent the potential misuse of such knowledge.

These two terms, esoteric and occult, if defined as something that deals with hidden forces of nature is equated to magic in everyday conversation and in many dictionaries. Magic is an older term, harder to define. It is derived from Old Persian word *magush*, possibly from the root *magh-* meaning to be able, to have

---

58 Online Etymology Dictionary: http://etymonline.com/index.php?allowed_in_frame=0&search=esoteric (May/12/2017)

power.[59] Greek word *magos*, from which the modern word magic probably stems and had spread through the Europe, has the same origin. The word *magos* in ancient Greece referred to the magi, students of Zarathustra who had similar social status as that of the Brahman in India, in their respective period of time. The magi were considered a priestly class or caste which was considered to have spiritual and material power.[60]

Based on the meaning of the word *magush* and the description of the magi, the original meaning of the word magic is probably power or spiritual power. Some authors of books on "magic" or "occultism" prefer the term magic (i.e. Bardon and Carroll) taking into consideration its original meaning. Serous practitioners consider magic a spiritual practice which primarily serves to expand one's consciousness, to gain knowledge, and for the ultimate purpose of self-improvement.

This practice is sometimes called Spiritual Alchemy because it deals with transformation of mind/spirit rather than matter. Hermeticism, tradition to which Bardon belonged, and Chinese Chi Gong (Chi Cultivation) are such practices. It is a question whether the "occult phenomena" described in such texts is merely a metaphor for spiritual development, rather than literal

---

59 Online Etymology Dictionary: http://etymonline.com/index.php?allowed_in_frame=0&search=magic (May/12/2017)
60 Veljačić, Č. 1979, *Filozofija istočnih naroda II*, Matica hrvatska, Zagreb p. 12

description of a real phenomena. Spiritual practice needs not be something mystical, but quite the opposite if spirit is considered the same, or at least similar and related in any way to human mind. The expansion of consciousness can be considered as expansion of the scope of understanding. In fact, the practice of controlling emotions causes a more objective mentality which in turn has a similar effect of higher understanding.

This book is dedicated to the topic of mental discipline and as such it serves for self-improvement and betterment of the reader. Philosophy, mental techniques and exercises described here can change your perspective on many things. The resulting changes in the mentality and perspective, or even in the consciousness itself can be considered spiritual.

There are various occult, or magic traditions with ancient or more recent origin. There are many similarities between them in terms of cosmology, goals, ethics, methods, and the theory behind the practice of magic or occultism. Though they may seem contradictory in their teachings, when studied more thoroughly, a fundamental similarity can be seen: manipulation and perception of the subtle energy, called differently but defined almost the same in all of them. Some of the names for the subtle energy are Psi, Chi, Ki, Kia, Mana, Prana, Bio-energy, etc. Most of them mean life force in their respective languages. It will be called simply energy, or subtle energy in this book. Subtle energy is the term used by online community of occult enthusiasts under the name of Psionism. In this and older systems, it is usually defined as a universal force available to everyone. It is not considered something like a deity, but a natural occurrence. The properties of subtle energy change according to the environment and the consciousness of living beings. Unfocused thoughts cause insignificant change in the ambiance, while focused thoughts can theoretically cause a noticeable change.

Franz Bardon defines it in terms of traditional elements: fire, water, air, and earth which all emanate from the fifth element Akasha, or Ether.[61] His system is a combination of eastern spiritual practices, hence the term "Akasha", and western alchemy and practice of magic. He also figuratively describes the behavior of energy as electric and magnetic. Magnetism symbolizes passive and attractive properties of energy, while electricity symbolizes active properties.[62] The practice is not different from other systems. Apparent division of energy in elements is more conceptual than substantial. The division can be primarily considered as different ways to apply the same energy. His techniques consist of direct control of energy by means of user's will, similar to those described by Psions. As such they are very useful for the purpose of this book. But Bardon does not describe

61 Bardon, F., 2018, *Initiation Into Hermetics*, Merkur Publishing, USA, p. 26
62 Ibid. p. 31-36

the methods to sense energy as Psions do. It is instead implied through the use of visualizations in the practice of Magic.

In Peter Carroll's system energy is called Kia, but the concept is somewhat different from the former systems. It is described as ego or consciousness. It can also be called spirit, lifeforce, or soul. Kia is a part of a larger lifeforce of the universe. As such it can be used to influence the realization of possibilities in a way favorable to the user. Everything originates from Chaos, which here is a term equivalent to a deity, or Logos from ancient Greek philosophy. Chaos cannot be known directly, but through Ether. Ether is defined as entirety of possibilities made by Chaos. These possibilities come into physical existence naturally according to natural laws and probability. However, a magician can influence the possibilities to his favor through Kia.[63] Carroll does not describe directly willpower based techniques for use of magic. Instead his methods rely on rituals, sigils, and mantra. The former two come close to willpower based techniques similar to those of the Psions and Bardon. As such his techniques are not as useful for the purpose of this book. However, the reader may or may not believe in the truthfulness of their magic teachings, but it is certain that people like Bardon and Carroll offer excellent meditation techniques and possess astonishing insight into human psychology. This makes their works invaluable for personal

63 Carroll, P., 1987, *Liber Null*, Weiser Books, San Francisco, p. 28-30

development.

Despite the fact that occult systems are often connected to religion, under assumption that the theory is true to any extent, it is wrong to say that occult practice is exclusively religious. It is a skill, just like meditation, and it can be used by anyone, separate of any form of ideological or religious views. Some religions prohibit the use of these and similar techniques, like they prohibit meditation. This prohibition is either based in doctrine, or just a means to divert their followers from competition. Practitioners of such religions should consider giving up one or the other. The difference between occultism and religion in practice is in the fact that religious people perform rituals and pray blindly for a result to manifest from a mystical source, while in occultism one consciously causes the desired result according to natural laws. This means that, contrary to the popular belief, occultism or magic is not about mysticism, but rather demystifying what is considered to be mystical and miraculous.

The use of such techniques is also considered and defined as supernatural. Supernatural means something above the nature in general, or superior to one's nature. If by the term supernatural is implied above nature in general, it means that supernatural can not exist, because there can be nothing "above" nature, that defies its laws. If it is implied above human nature, it means impossible for humans. In that case humans would be unable to use such techniques and would be unaware of their existence.

None of the occult systems define their practice as supernatural. In fact, they all assume the existence of, and describe the natural laws which make it possible, as stated previously. It would be too great a digression to describe such theories in detail. For this book the only important fact is the existence of such techniques, not details and mechanisms behind them. If the reader is interested in studying the more advanced systems, they can read some of the numerous works on the topic. However, they should keep in mind that there are no "magic" words that take problems away. One will gain little or nothing without hard work. Moreover, they may gain little or nothing *despite* hard work.[64]

Proving to others the existence of subtle energy and the possibility of perceiving and manipulating it is a hard and futile endeavor. Some people will stubbornly deny it with or without potential evidence, while others will accept it without a second thought. There are many videos of people claiming to be able to perform actions like psychokinesis or clairvoyance, but knowing the modern technology it is very easy to fake it. It may be the best to try to prove, or disprove it for one's self, by experimenting

64 Bardon, F., 2018, *Initiation Into Hermetics,* Merkur Publishing, USA, p. 17

under a reasonable criteria for that purpose, because using an unreliable method can easily lead to self deception. In addition, it is useless trying to impress others with your occult abilities, because they will always assume there is trickery involved. Trickery really is the best option for entertainment. If one wishes to find the truth behind occult practice, it is the best to do it yourself, if it is considered to be worth the effort.

It is important to take into consideration that these instructions are not enough for further experimentation. Their purpose is only to develop minimum level of skill required for manipulating emotions. Described techniques are primarily inspired by techniques mentioned at Shifted Perspectives website[65] and in Franz Bardon's *"Initiation Into Hermetics"*. They are described as originally intended for sake of completion and to honor the sources. As it was mentioned, it is only important to use the methods to learn willpower based control of emotions.

The practice as described in the present work is primarily based on Psionism. As it was said, they are a community of occult enthusiasts who gather on online forums. As such, their doctrine has the same problem as Wikipedia: anyone can write the material. This makes it questionable to what degree is it written

---

65 The site was shut down during the writing of this book. However, similar material can be found on other sites.

by serious and knowledgeable practitioners. In comparison to individuals like Carroll and Bardon who, if nothing else, exhibit philosophic wisdom and insight, there is less than 1% of people among the Psions for whom could be said the same. Given the subjective nature of occult/magic practice, Psionic techniques have obvious weaknesses. For that reason it is the best to treat them as an exercise for channeling your will, not an example of serious practice of magic.

Another way to understand or interpret these techniques could be to take them as a concept or a method of self-hypnosis. Perception and manipulation of subtle energy taken as a mental exercise or meditation used to deepen the control and understanding of emotions and instincts. Readers who do not care for proving or disproving occult techniques taken literally can still benefit from their use as described here. Which interpretation is correct, literal or non literal, is irrelevant as long as the techniques work to shape one's own subjective reality at will. Because, "even a slight ability to change oneself is more valuable than any power over the external universe."[66] Readers who are absolutely uninterested in these topics should skip to the epilogue with the authors best wishes.

---

66 Carroll, P., 1987, *Liber Null*, Weiser Books, San Francisco, p. 16

Energy manipulation

On criteria for experiments

The mentioned criteria for experimenting with occult practice with the aim of proving, or disproving it to one's self should be something that prevents confirmation bias, self-deception and similar errors. For example, if you are experimenting with a thermometer and trying to make it change the temperature with your mind, it must be done in external conditions that will not change its temperature themselves. This means you cannot touch it and it cannot be in a room with unstable temperature. You must also avoid optical illusions, such as parallax errors in reading the measurement. It could be avoided by using digital thermometer or placing a camera to record it during the experiment.

Another important factor in experiments is its reproduction. If you cannot reproduce the results of the experiment consistently, it means that there is either a problem in the procedure or that the experiment disproves the theory. In natural sciences experiments done correctly will always produce the same result regardless of what you may think of it, but in occultism experiment depends on the mental state. If the practitioner is doubtful, excited, unfocused, or otherwise disturbed he will not be able to perform the experiment correctly. This means that mental state is an important factor to take into consideration. Moreover, if you attempt to do an experiment while you lack the required skill, it is impossible to succeed in the first place. Natural sciences are purely objective, while occult practices depend on the subjective which can make the experiments highly unreliable.

These are just a few ideas to help the curious, but the experimentation of this type is not directly important for this book so it will not be expanded further. The indirect benefit of the experimentation is in the development of mental discipline while practicing during the experiment.

Basic energy manipulation

Before explaining its application on emotion control, it is necessary to explain energy manipulation itself. As defined by Psions, energy manipulation is the act of using the energy for a specific goal. The act of determining this goal, or "instructing" the energy what to do is called programming. It is the act of imprinting one's will or intention into the energy. Here it will be explained how to use the energy manipulation without going into details of mechanics behind the energy manipulation, specifically how is it possible to perceive and manipulate energy in the first place. In fact, as it was mentioned before, it is not even important for this book if it is really possible or not.

First step required to manipulate energy is to learn how to feel its presence in your body. For that purpose, relax and concentrate on the general feeling of your body. Mentally observe your limbs and torso. Feel their warmth and try to detect the subtle, non physical feeling "behind" it.

Another method is to visualize the energy flowing through you and trying to feel it. There is no need to force the feeling, just relax and observe. Gradually you will notice the difference between the physical sensation of the body and the subtle energy. Once you become aware of it, with a little practice, it will become as easy as breathing to feel the energy at will. The specific feeling is different for everyone so there is no purpose in trying to describe it.

To get a better feeling of the energy, try moving it in a hand and feel it accumulating there. To do it, visualize the energy moving towards it and gathering there. Any visualization will do because energy follows the intention, while visualization itself serves as a tool to make the process easier.

Another method for moving the energy without visualization is by tactile feeling. It is done by sensing the energy in your body, focusing your attention on the point where you want to move it, and willing it to move. In some occult traditions abdomen is used as the initial point of energy. When moving the energy in a body part, at the beginning it may be easier to draw the energy from there and focus it elsewhere.

After gathering the energy in a hand, try gathering it in the other hand. Next gather it in a foot, then the other foot. Try focusing it in both hands or both feet simultaneously. Next try moving the energy from one hand to the other, from one foot to the other. A way to do this is by visualizing the energy moving from one point to another. Another way, by the tactile feeling of the energy, is done by focusing on the starting point and the destination point while willing the energy to move.

Thinking about moving the energy and actually doing it is different. It is necessary to invest an amount of mental work in case of *doing*, which is not required in case of thinking alone. The difference is easily learned by practice and experience. These exercises will familiarize you with a new way to channel your will and to move your awareness across your body. It will be explained later how to use them to control your emotions.

The energy can be focused in any body part, or in multiple body parts at the same time by using these techniques. Practice moving the energy throughout the body until you can do it easily at will. Energy manipulation requires a certain amount of mental effort, just like other mental activities, like studying or meditation. Prolonged use of energy manipulation will make the user mentally tired. Overdoing it is counterproductive just like overdoing physical exercises.

At this point one may think that the feeling of energy is a product of auto-suggestion, or that it is the feeling of blood circulation, but as one practices and experiments with the energy it becomes harder to discard it as such. While positive effects can be a placebo because they are the goal of the practice, side effects occur regardless of subjects knowledge on them, which is an argument for techniques being real. Whatever the truth is, you cannot be certain until you can produce a measurable physical effect. The reader is free to decide for themselves what to think. This can be considered a weakness of the Psionic system. The systems of Bardon and Carroll do not rely on sensing the energy, so it is not a problem for them. From the perspective of a practitioner of magic, focusing on the feeling of energy by training to make it stronger can be a distraction from more beneficial forms of exercise. Namely, meditation and other forms of mental training which build a strong foundation necessary for magic practice, instead of starting with the practice itself and simultaneously building the foundation as described by the Psions.

Moving the energy to the outside of the body can be done by

means of the same methods. The difference is in the fact that it is not as easy to feel the energy outside as it is inside the body, which makes it harder to determine if you are successful. This can be achieved by turning the attention from observing the energy inside, to the outside. For the purpose of this book it is enough to be familiar with the concept. Just having a rough feeling for it will suffice to use the technique for control of emotions.

A method for the practice:

Feel the energy inside your body. Observe it with your mind, then slowly move your attention from the inside of the body outwards. Observe the feeling on top of your skin and feel the energy there. Now try to observe the space around you with your mind. There is no need to actively search for the energy, just relax and observe. Gradually you should be able to feel it in your surroundings.

Visualizations can be of use to make the process easier: Imagine the energy filling the space around you, then try to feel that energy. Observe it with your mind with the intention of sensing the energy. Imagine a wave of light emitted from your body that scans the surrounding energy in all directions like a sonar, or a wide ray of light that scans a desired direction. Any visualization can help if it makes the concept easier to comprehend.

Like other mental techniques, this can be done in many ways. Described techniques are just examples of basic ones that serve as guidelines to help at the beginning. The user can change them as it suits their needs. They can also invent completely new ones or find other techniques elsewhere. The specific one chosen does not matter as long as it serves the purpose.

There are two simple techniques used for expelling the energy:

1. Breathing out the energy: This technique is a combination of Psionic and Bardon's[67] techniques. It is performed by synchronizing breathing, more specifically, breathing out with moving the energy out of the body. To do so relax, take a deep breath, and slowly breathe out. Feel the energy in your body and while breathing out, imagine it moving outwards into your surroundings. Try doing this with the entire surface of the skin. The same can be done without visualizations, simply by feeling the energy in your body and willing it to move to your surroundings while you breathe out. In both cases, with or without the aid of visualization, feeling and observing the energy

---

67 Bardon, F., 2018, *Initiation Into Hermetics*, Merkur Publishing, USA, p. 101-106

in and out of the body, as described before, will help determine if you are successful. If successful you should feel the movement of the energy outwards as it leaves your body. If there is no energy movement, focus first on moving the energy and secondly on breathing. This may happen if you are only focusing on the action of breathing while the focus on energy manipulation is lacking, thus making it ineffective.

2. Grounding: This technique is called thus because it is performed by sending energy into the ground. To do so, feel the energy in your body, then imagine it moving to your feet, and then into the ground like roots of a tree. Obviously, it does not matter if you are on the ground floor or not because the energy will be moved out of the body regardless of your location in space. The primary purpose of this technique is to get rid of excess energy that can accumulate in the body during exercises of energy manipulation. It is essentially the same as the previous technique, just expressed through a different concept.

Energy can also be focused in something specific or in an empty space by focusing on the chosen destination while breathing out the energy instead of just expelling it outwards. To focus the energy into a point in space or in an existing object, focus on a chosen destination and imagine the energy moving

265

there from your body. This can also be synchronized with breathing if the user finds it easier. As you breathe out focus on the object and will the energy move into it. If visualizations help, image the energy moving into the object.

Using energy for a specific purpose or just expelling it depletes the user. In that case they will find it hard or impossible to use energy manipulation until energy is restored. Depletion can be prevented by drawing in the energy from the surroundings or by using the outside energy directly. Drawing in more energy than the body can handle is harmful. If there is not too much excess energy, problems like headache, insomnia, anxiety, lack of concentration, and similar may occur. Using a technique to expel the excess energy will solve the problem. If there is too much excess energy, more serious problems can arise. Such problems can damage one's progress in mental exercises, just like physical overexertion damages progress in physical abilities. Both are painful and unhealthy.

To prevent depletion and excess energy at the beginning of development in energy manipulation, it is enough not to work too hard. When you feel tired stop the exercise and rest until you are comfortable to continue. More advanced practitioners of energy manipulation can maintain the balance of energy by keeping track of energy spent and absorbed. To do it effectively, you need to learn your limits by experience. Resting is the simplest way to replenish the spent energy. Absorbing it from the outside is quicker, but it tires the user so it cannot be used constantly. When skilled enough, it is possible to estimate the state of energy in the body by introspection.

For the purpose of this book, it is enough to know how to imprint intention into the energy and use it as such. More specifically, it is only necessary to develop a feeling for the procedure so that you can later implement it to control emotions. In magic theory, any intention can be imprinted into the energy while focusing it: to heal, to damage, to warm up, to cool, etc. but effects depend on how skilled the user is. When energy is used on self, the effects are easily felt. But it takes practice to make a significant difference such as to heal an injury, to warm up or to cool down a room, and similar feats that can be observed by anyone. It may prove difficult even to make a noticeable change on a thermometer, but succeeding in that intention is a first step towards greater ability.

Drawing energy from the surroundings can be done by using the opposite technique of breathing out the energy. Energy can also be drawn from a specific object or from general surroundings. This skill is more useful for magic practices than for this book as we will mostly either transform or expel undesirable emotions or instincts. However, it is useful for practice and as a balance to the opposite techniques.

Two simple techniques for absorbing energy:

1. Breathing in the energy: This technique is opposite to the one for expelling energy. To draw the energy from your surroundings, feel the outside energy and imagine it flowing into your body as you breathe in. Imagine your surroundings to be a vast mass of energy and visualizing a part of that energy flowing into you. The same result can be accomplished by the tactile feeling, without relying on visualization. When doing this exercise try to absorb the energy with the entire surface of the skin. Both methods can be combined to make the process more effective.

When practicing this skill, according to Bardon[68], beginners should not absorb more than 20-30 consecutive breaths of energy. At their level it is easy to draw in too much as their body is not used to such exercises. When you reach the chosen number, for example 5 breaths are counted, it is necessary to breathe out the same amount of energy as it was previously described or to spend it on training. A good way to practice without overloading is to

---
68   Ibid. p. 50-51

breathe the energy in and out alternatively. With such breathing exercises quality comes before quantity. It is much more effective to breathe deeply and naturally with a strong intention, rather than forcing the air in to the limits of your lungs. The exercise is not about the air itself, but the intention behind the procedure.

2. Drawing energy from a specific point: This is done by focusing on an object, feeling the energy in it and visualizing the energy flowing from it towards you. Imagining the energy in the object and the flow of energy towards you can make it easier.

With this technique it is not as easy to keep track of the amount of energy absorbed. To avoid overloading one should absorb small amounts until they learn their limits. Excess energy can be disposed of by means of previously mentioned methods.

Energy can be manipulated by relying on imagination as a helping tool or simply by willpower alone, depending on personal preference. There is no need for supporting actions like body gestures, postures, breathing exercises, and similar. The support can be of use, but if you are unable to use it for some reason the effectiveness of your techniques will be reduced.

Application of energy manipulation on emotion control

Sensing, programming, absorbing, and focusing the energy are the basics of the energy manipulation. In this system emotions behave in similar manner as subtle energy. They can be felt and manipulated the same way. The only difference is in the fact that everyone can feel emotions without training, which is not the case with energy. In this manual it will be described how to use this similarity between emotions and subtle energy to subjugate emotions to mind to a higher degree than what was done with the techniques of the previous chapter, thus bringing mental discipline to a higher level.

The same methods for emotion control are valid for control of instincts and urges. For the sake of simplicity only the use of techniques for control of emotions will be described, while the same techniques can be used on instincts as well. Some of them are biological necessities like thirst and hunger, so they are harder to control than emotions. They can be reduced so they can be easier to ignore until they can be satisfied. Other non essential instincts that one may have, such as aggression, irritability, sex drive etc. can be controlled to a much higher degree depending on mental discipline, personal interest, and philosophy. The two strongest instincts and the hardest to control are fear and sex drive. Fear is essential for self preservation and as such must never be fully extinguished, but only conquered so that it does not control you. Sex drive is essential for the preservation of the species. It is especially strong in men and it is the reason they often do self destructive actions just for a chance of satisfying this instinct. For this reason, if it is not possible to extinguish it, the sex drive must be kept on short leash, otherwise you risk being on the leash yourself.

Emotion control techniques:

The first method to control emotions with the use of energy manipulation is to cancel out unwanted emotions with energy. For that purpose it is enough to feel the emotion in question and focus the energy on it with the intention of canceling it. The amount of energy used should be just slightly above the energy of the emotion itself. Suffocating emotions like that creates energy leftovers that can cause problems similar to those of excess energy, with the difference of affecting only parts of the body instead of affecting the entire system. These remains do not cause the same problems as mentioned before, but their presence can be felt and it can be distracting. For that reason this method should be used only if no other method works. The problem is solved by expelling this form of excess energy, but the simplest way is to avoid the problem in the first place.

The second method is to focus on the unwanted emotion and feel its energy. Instead of letting the emotion control you, disperse its energy across the body. That energy can be used for energy manipulation in general, to fuel your current activity, or any other purpose. This is done by visualizing emotions and urges as energy. However it feels the most natural: in form of electricity, light, fire, etc. Feel these unwanted emotions in their new form and imagine them flowing throughout your body energizing you, making you stronger. The aim is to take direct control of the phenomena (emotions, urges, instincts) by associating them with an appropriate idea. Through this idea you abstract the emotions in your mind so that their hold over you is relaxed. They will no longer be an intense drive, but they will change in a form of tame energy, for the lack of better word, which can be resisted and controlled more easily.

In terms of occultism, this method basically converts energy of the emotions into raw energy, disassembling the emotion and re-purposing its potential. To be more specific, for example if angered in sparring, the anger can be transformed into subtle energy that can be directed into arms and legs and used in a less volatile form to boost your abilities. Regarding the boosting of current activities, distracting emotions and instincts when converted into energy can be used to focus on your work, occult or physical exercises, studying, reading, etc.

The third method is to simply expel the energy of emotions using one of the previously described techniques. This avoids the problems of the first method and releases the excess energy in the same time. This method relies on the same concept as the previous one. The same visualizations can be used to observe emotions and instincts as energy. The main difference is how you deal with it afterwards. In this method you expel it from your body instead of using it. It is particularly useful when you find yourself in a situation that causes a lot of unwanted emotions. If the energy converted from emotions is not needed for any purpose it is best to simply dispose of it.

The first and simplest technique for expelling emotions as energy was already mentioned before in a different way. Focus on the unwanted emotion, observe it with your mind, and imagine it as energy, steam, air, or a mass of black smoke. Take a deep breath and exhale it like it was said before. Try to make the visualization as clear as possible. Imagine it vividly to the best of your abilities, then as you exhale imagine the energy rushing out of your body in the imagined form. The stronger your focus the more effective the will technique be. This exercise is very simple and practical. It does not require too strong concentration or too much time for effective use. When you get used to it you will be able to vent out strong emotions with ease.

The second technique consists of imagining the inside of your body as a mass of bright light, and unwanted emotions as dark stains in the light. Focus on these stains and connect them mentally as an idea with your unwanted emotions and instincts. As you breathe in imagine the bright light flowing into you and clearing up these stains, leaving only inner peace or positive emotions, depending on the personal preference. It is a variation of the previous exercise. They can be used alternatively for a continuous effect: breathing in white, clean light and breathing out black smoke. This makes it more versatile for everyday use. It is more complex than the previous exercise so it is more suitable for meditation than use on the move, but it can still be used that way.

Another generally useful skill worth mentioning is isolating your mind from outside influences. It is used when you are in extraordinarily tense situation: whether it is self defense, or a socially awkward situation when mediocre people are pressuring you and shaming you to conform to their way of thinking, or a debate with a particularly annoying person who uses underhand tactics to provoke you, if you get injured in an accident, or something similar. In such a case clear your mind and focus, reflect on what are you doing there and what is your goal. Use all the mental strength you acquired by training and keep your guard up. This can be reinforced by whatever visualization you see fit. The simplest method may be to maintain awareness of your body and surroundings, and to think only about what is important at the moment so are not easily thrown out of balance. The intense mental focus on the purpose or the action itself shields the mind from outside influences and prevents overwhelming emotions caused by a sudden problem.

It can also be achieved by focusing all your mental strength into the intention to remain firm and defiant despite the outside influence. You block out all the emotional and physical discomfort by force of your will. In unexpected situations like these your principles and strength of character are tested. A banal example is when you are watching a horror movie and you expect a jump scare, so you make your inner state unchangeable by "holding" it firm with your will. It is similar to maintaining the visualization during meditation. The exact way you go about using this technique depends on the situation.

When one becomes proficient in the use of these techniques, they will surely notice that the feeling of emotions is generally different than before. Emotions will feel more like programmed subtle energy than a mystical unexplainable phenomenon, as average people see it. Emotions of greater intensity may feel like a mass of energy which is more like a waste and annoyance than something desirable. Also the point in the body where you feel emotions may change depending on how you manipulate their energy. This is not strange because emotions are rally felt in the brain, not elsewhere in the body.

The key to success with these techniques is persistence and focus. Pay attention to the process as you practice. You must learn to influence an emotion with willpower as if using a mental muscle. Similar to learning the difference between auto-suggestion and a simple thought, shaping emotions at will can be learned by practice and experimentation. Once you find the mental mechanism in your mind it is just a matter of practice to achieve the results you aim for.

It is important to notice the similarity between these techniques and meditation: emotions themselves become the object of focus, so the thoughts that cause their formation are blocked. The re-formation of these emotions is blocked because their cause is removed. It is replaced by the new intention, the intense mental focus on this intention, and the goal. This gives the idea how emotions form and how can they be effectively canceled. Exercises with re-purposing the emotion and perceiving it as if it was energy helps to develop the skill of shaping them at will, as if moving a hand. It becomes as easy as that, so it does not require much effort or support actions like visualizations.

With the help of these skills emotions must be prevented from influencing one's actions. If undisciplined emotions are compared to a storm, one must strive to remain in the eye of the storm and thus unaffected. Emotions must become a tool that serves the user, not a mystical unexplainable force that governs their actions contrary to their will. Emotions must feel like a mental object that can be grasped and shaped by the users mental hand. This feeling is developed through the described exercises.

For example, if you are in a battle, whether it is a sparring practice, competition, or a self defense situation. Even in the situation of a debate or dealing with difficult people as mention in the first chapter, the rules are the same. Emotions and instincts that may arise in that situation such as fear, anger, shame, guilt, or aggressiveness must not control you. Emotions must be first observed objectively with your mind, along with their effect on your behavior, then reshaped or destroyed depending on your preference. If the person wants to consider emotions to be energy, they must be used as such. This is done by keeping the intention in mind instead of losing yourself in the urges caused by emotions. For example to charge in like a rabid animal and hit the opponent with full force. The intention is always to maintain the control of the situation. Energy provided by the emotion, whether it is produced naturally or induced by the previously mentioned methods must be focused in the limbs and body and used as an incentive and as fuel to block, strike, and evade when necessary, never losing your focus and control in the process. If it is not needed, their energy should be dispersed as described before. In essence, energy of emotion must be considered as something physical and separate from the mind which governs actions. Energy is used when needed and while needed, and then discarded afterwards if it cannot be saved for later use.

Another mentioned example of maintaining control is a debate. One side in the discussion will often try to provoke various emotions in their opponent such as anger, guilt, shame, etc. to throw them out of balance so they can use invalid arguments without detection. In that case one must always keep calm and must never let emotions make them react angrily and lose sight of the discussed topic and arguments used. The calm and rationality can be easily maintained if one trains themselves not to react emotionally, at least in debates if not when dealing with people in general. Emotional reactions are just a bad habit. People often react harshly by instinct to protect their pride, even though it is completely unnecessary. The same can be said about everyday situations when dealing with difficult people, as mentioned in the previous chapters. If your passive indifference is lacking in the debate, you can always take control "by force" like in the previous example. Instead of dispersing the energy of emotions throughout your body to fuel your abilities, expel it to the outside. This will give you an opportunity to compose yourself.

These techniques are not hard to learn and develop if basics of what was said in this, and the previous chapters are kept in mind. If used frequently they are easy to perfect. The training starts from everyday situations and later progresses towards more difficult situations.

As you use these techniques over a long period of time they will become easy and natural. The original exercises used to develop them will gradually fade from the use leaving only pure willpower based control of emotions. At that point it is no longer as necessary to rely visualization or the energy manipulation exercises. Controlling emotions with your will becomes a true mental ability which seems not developed by training but inborn. This ability is the true goal of this chapter. However, to remain disciplined and to achieve a high level of passive indifference personal development through meditation and philosophy is inevitable.

Further explanation of the concept of energy manipulation

Application of the energy manipulation on the emotion control does not make the previous methods obsolete, but rather extends them. In fact, personal philosophy, meditation, and self-hypnosis remain the main tools for mental discipline. Willpower based control of emotions is just another tool that allows higher flexibility of previous techniques, and reduces dependence on meditation.

Willpower is improved with the practice of energy manipulation. This manifests on self-hypnosis as increased effectiveness and success rate of its use. At the beginning only self-hypnosis used deliberately will be enhanced. Later the will of the user will manifest automatically. This means that intention alone without specific self-hypnosis techniques will activate the desired effect. In that case, if one focuses on an emotion with the intention of removing it, the emotion will be removed. This is caused by the increased control of thoughts. As mention before, emotions are caused primarily by thought process. Your emotions arise depending on what and how you think about something. Negative thoughts cause negative emotions, while positive thoughts cause positive emotions. Thoughts can arise spontaneously by following a train of thoughts, from subconsciousness, or triggered by outside influences.

When you focus on an emotion, emotion itself becomes the object of thought. In the process, the former thought that created it in the first place is replaced. Thus the emotion loses its cause and ceases to exist, as it was mentioned. This is achieved through simple objective introspection. It is the product of the practice of meditation and energy manipulation.

Removing the thought directly will work as described in the previous chapter, but increased mental discipline will make it easier to perform. If the intention is to augment the emotion while focusing on it, it is necessary to maintain the thought that caused it in the first place and add mental energy from the intention, which happens automatically. This is essentially a combination of the previous techniques with the new way of focusing your will described in this chapter.

At this stage of expertise, as mentioned in the previous chapter, one is capable of surpassing or casting aside certain concepts. Energy manipulation provides the means through which the mind can directly influence emotion or instinct. That means is the subtle energy in the literal interpretation of magic theory. In non literal interpretation this means is the action of willpower through control of emotions and instincts by associating them with ideas.

It allows the will to manifest automatically by shaping the inner state of the user as they desire. Changing the inner state at will is the expression of mental discipline.

Control of emotions through meditation and self-hypnosis is more suitable for shaping one's own personality and general disposition towards concepts and everyday situations. Discipline of thoughts and energy manipulation are more suitable to maintain what was achieved with meditation and to control the changes of inner state that occur in everyday life. Shaping emotions, or rather the inner state at will as described here is the goal of this chapter. It could be achieved with techniques from previous chapters, but it is more on point and deliberate through exercises from this one.

The practice of mentioned abilities produces a form of introspection otherwise inaccessible. In combination with meditation and contemplation it gives access to subconsciousness. Once the subconscious is rendered conscious, it will no longer be able to control the individual, and *it* can be controlled instead. Control of the subconsciousness allows one to change their personality as they see fit, as it was mentioned in the previous chapter.

Better introspection also helps one to examine and feel their body more accurately which allows better control over it. When one is used to monitoring their body and mind through introspection, it becomes very easy to notice abnormalities caused by food, drink, illness, or any other negative influence on the health of the individual.

Despite superiority of human intellect to that of other animals, humans are still highly influenced by subconscious processes which, along with conscious though, form instincts, urges, and emotions. To gain a higher degree of free will, or the true free will one needs to conquer the animalistic part of human nature and live in accordance with reason. This is certainly achievable by an individual, but not by the collective. The society in general may only become more rational if the evolution leads naturally in that direction. Before that point in time, true freedom is reserved only for those who are willing to work for it and can become immune to the harmful outside influence of the society.

A light trance that is induced by using mental skills described here can cause slower reactions. To avoid this it is necessary to maintain relaxed awareness and focus. If one is lost in thought or focused on introspection when it is necessary to react, for example to catch or hit the ball in the game or to avoid or block an attack in martial arts, their reactions will activate too late. If they maintain awareness of their surroundings, not only it is possible to react naturally, but also to use the quick mind to speed up reactions. Quick reactions are common characteristic of sportsmen. They are gained by experience and long training. With mental discipline reactions improved by training can be enhanced even further.

The focus alone gained by meditation exercises and energy manipulation are intertwined in the effort of controlling your emotions. It may be difficult to distinguish between their effects. With experience and frequent use of the techniques described in this book it will become clear that they are incomplete if limited to the use of only one or the other. Using the all three described methods of manipulating emotions, namely rationalization, self-hypnosis, and energy manipulation, combined with philosophic mentality, thought control and increased willpower give access to mental abilities that can together be called mental discipline. The aim of this manual is to provide instructions to develop these skills and the resulting mental discipline. It is up to the reader to decide to what degree will they develop each of these skills and mental discipline in general.

Epilogue

The purpose for the described mental discipline and the control of emotions is not necessarily to block out and destroy emotions in every single situation, but only in those situations that make one do self destructive actions. There were many examples of such actions throughout the book.

Another important point to consider is that mental discipline is not meant only for "damage management" in an emotionally difficult situation, but as a permanent shield. To achieve this it is important, as mentioned before, to develop a mentality that promotes strength of character and self confidence. True self confidence can only arise from continuous self improvement, not from an inflated ego and self deception.

If we imagine difficult situations as a deep water that, in an extreme case, suffocates with overwhelming emotions, the mental discipline is the ability to pull your head out and take a deep breath. More importantly, in everyday life people find themselves in doubt, confused over which action to take, which path to follow. The choice is clouded with emotions because there are many things at stake. Mental discipline helps to clear your mind so that you can rationally choose what is the best. It allows you to distance yourself so that you can see the whole picture. Emotions are mainly directed to most immediate and basest of needs and wants. In order to be wise, one must learn not to rely on them when making important decisions in life. It is wise to sacrifice the immediate pleasure for greater gain later.

Described techniques allow a wide range of emotion manipulation. What degree of emotional intensity or potential is to be limited depends on personal goals and preferences. The question is: what does one wishes to accomplish and how much is he willing to sacrifice?

Mental discipline and control of thoughts and emotions are an important prerequisite of some occult systems. The present work can be of great use in combination with such books that discuss primarily the occult theory and practice (i.e. Initiation Into Hermetics, Liber Null), because it treats the topic of mental discipline as the primary topic, with more detail.

Do not throw away your life, my fellow man. Do not blindly chase what others say will bring you happiness. Do not derive your self-worth and self-respect on an external source. Let them be determined from the inside, based on your own philosophy. Do not let anyone tell you what is a "real man". Do not forget your self-interest and your goals, your *Opus Magnum*. Be disciplined, strong, defiant, and proud.

Finally, here is a sonnet dedicated to Friedrich Nietzsche whose philosophy is an important inspiration for this book and the sonnet itself. There are two hidden references to Nietzsche's quotes in the text. Furthermore, the sonnet is dedicated to all other mentors, teachers, professors etc. who give us the most beautiful gift of inspiration and wisdom. It is based on the contents of this book and it is not about a woman and tragic love. That is just a mask for the true meaning, a touch of classic poetry.

Sofia

Mi hai portato la luce nella vita
Col suo sorriso quanto dolce tanto
amaro. È la conoscenza mai vista
il ciò su che si fonda nostro rapporto.

Ma prima di raggiungerti è perduta
la mia strada. Ti cerco dappertutto,
sei tu il pensiero che mi tormenta
in solitudine, frutto mai provato.

Puzzano ancora i corpi dei bruciati
Vivi dentro il fuoco illuminante

Cercato dagli studiosi brillanti.

Sul cuore mi sei un carico pesante.
Non posso portarti neanche lasciarti.
A metà di via tra noi c'è la morte.

Sources

Books:

Aristotel, 2001, *Metafizika*, Signum, Zagreb

Aristotel, 1988, *Nikomahova etika*, Globus, Zagreb

Aurelius, M., 2003, *Meditations*, Modern Library, New York

Bardon, F., 2018, *Initiation Into Hermetics*, Merkur Publishing, USA

Carroll, P. J., 1987, *Liber Null*, Weiser Books, San Francisco, CA

Copleston, F., 1993, *A History of Philosophy Vol. 1*, Image Books, New York

Miyamoto, M., 2018, *The Book of Five Rings*, Tuttle publishing, Boston

Nietzsche, F., 2013, *Al di là del bene e del male*, Adelphi, Milano

Nietzsche, F., 1972, *Twilight Of The Idols*, The Viking Press, New York

Platon, 2002, *Država*, BIGZ, Beograd

Veljačić, Č.,1983, *Filozofija istočnih naroda I*, Matica Hrvatska, Zagreb

Veljačić, Č., 1979, *Filozofija istočnih naroda II*, Matica hrvatska, Zagreb

Other sources:

Internet Encyclopedia of Philosophy: https://www.iep.utm.edu/

Merriam-Webster Dictionary: https://www.merriam-webster.com/

Online Etymology Dictionary: http://www.etymonline.com/

Stanford Encyclopedia of Philosophy: https://plato.stanford.edu/index.html

Star Wars: Knights of the Old Republic, BioWare, LucasArts, 2003, video game

Vampire: The Masquerade – Bloodlines, Activision, Troika, 2004, video game